EDEXCEL GCSE IN BUSINESS UNIT 2: BUILDING A BUSINESS

Michelle Billington

Ian Marcousé

Louise Stubbs

658

Hodder Arnold
A MEMBER OF THE HODDER HEADLINE GROUP

Orders: please contact Bookpoint Ltd, 130 Milton Park, Abingdon, Oxon OX14 4SB. Telephone: (44) 01235 827720. Fax: (44) 01235 400454. Lines are open from 9.00–5.00, Monday to Saturday, with a 24-hour message answering service. You can also order through our website www.hoddereducation.co.uk

British Library Cataloguing in Publication Data
A catalogue record for this title is available from the British Library

ISBN: 978 0 340 94177 5

First Published 2007
Impression number   10 9 8 7 6 5 4 3 2
Year   2013 2012 2011 2010 2009 2008 2007

Cover photo © Luis Veiga/Photonica/Getty Images
Typeset by GreenGate Publishing Services, Tonbridge, Kent
Section opening pages by Ruth Thomlevold/NB Illustration
Illustrations by Barking Dog Art
Printed in Italy for Hodder Arnold, an imprint of Hodder Education and a member of the Hodder Headline Group, An Hachette Livre UK Company, 338 Euston Road, London NW1 3BH

Contents

Using this book

This book matches Unit 2 of the new Edexcel GCSE Business course. Building a Business is about the challenges of developing from a small firm into a medium-sized company. The book matches the course precisely, adding detail and life to the bare bones of the exam board specification. It does it by using the real stories of dozens of different companies, as they make daily decisions that affect the lives of staff and customers.

Just as with the Unit 1 book, the chapters are written to be read, not just used for reference. The Unit 2 exam requires you to make decisions, recommendations and judgements. The wider your knowledge of business, the easier it becomes to show these skills. So even if your teacher has not asked you to read a particular chapter, please do so. The more you read, the better your chance of a good grade. As with the Unit 1 book, the chapters are self-contained, so if you want to read chapter 13 before 12, that should not be a problem.

This new GCSE course has been designed to test your understanding of business more than your knowledge of facts. So the key to tackling the questions at the end of a chapter is to test your understanding. Do make sure to tackle the longer questions at the end of each chapter. Your teacher might not ask you to do this every time, but it is sensible for you to read the exercises and think about how to answer them. Your teacher will probably have the answer book, and could let you have a copy of the mark scheme for any question you have done.

The book is full of business stories, many of which are very recent. It would be wonderful, though, if you also read up-to-date stories in the day's papers. Try not to leave everything up to your teacher.

May I wish you every success with this book and with the course.

Ian Marcousé, co-author and series editor

Teachers

The book is accompanied by the Teacher's Resource, which includes answers to all the exercises. This is available from Hodder Arnold.

Acknowledgements

Michelle Billington: I would like to thank all of my 2006/2007 GCSE Applied Business students at Moor Park Business and Enterprise School. They helped research businesses that I could use for examples in the chapters and had a go at answering the end of unit questions. Special thanks go to Lauren, Shallom, Sara, Denny, Zaakir, Mubeen, Nirosa, Farheen, Huzaifa, Ben, both Muhammeds and both Ibrahims! Many thanks are also due to Ian Haslam for helping me put the chapters together.

Ian Marcousé: I owe a debt of gratitude to all the Pilot Centres who started the course in September 2006. Their enthusiasm was backed up by my 2006/2007 GCSE Business Studies students at Lambeth College. They patiently read chapters and tackled questions. Special mentions go to Chelsea, Raza and Duchoy, who all made an extra effort to provide feedback. At Hodder Arnold, Alexia Chan was the key figure in publishing books for the pilot, and Deborah Edwards did superbly at cajoling me into delivering on time.

Louise Stubbs: Many thanks to the GCSE Business students at Great Sankey High School for testing the exercises.

This material has been endorsed by Edexcel and offers high quality support for the delivery of Edexcel qualifications.

Edexcel endorsement does not mean that this material is essential to achieve any Edexcel qualification, nor does it mean that this is the only suitable material available to support any Edexcel qualification. No endorsed material will be used verbatim in setting any Edexcel examination and any resource lists produced by Edexcel shall include this and other appropriate texts. While this material has been through an Edexcel quality assurance process, all responsibility for the content remains with the publisher.

Copies of official specifications for all Edexcel qualifications may be found on the Edexcel website – www.edexcel.org.uk.

Every effort has been made to trace and acknowledge ownership of copyright. The publishers will be glad to make suitable arrangements with any copyright holders whom it has not been possible to contact. The authors and publishers would like to thank the following for the use of photographs in this volume:

Action Images/Lee Smith, p65; Alfred Pasieka/Science Photo Library, p23; Chinch Gryniewicz/Ecoscene/Corbis, p106; Craig Holmes/Alamy, p109; David Crausby/Alamy, p7; Glenn Dearing/eyevine, p66; ImageState/Alamy, p26; iStockphoto.com/Caziopeia, p96; iStockphoto.com/George Cairns, p76; iStockphoto.com/Graham Heywood, p71; iStockphoto.com/Joe Gough, p99; James Seddon/EggXactly Ltd, p33; Jim West/Alamy, p45; Kimberly White/Reuters/Corbis, p30; Mark Henley/Panos Pictures, p14; Matt Cardy/Getty Images, p69; Matt Hazell/First Light Solutions, p79; Metrow Foods (Grays) Ltd, p70; Phil Noble/PA Archive/PA Photos, p123; Rob Blackburn/photolibrary.com, p44; Thomas Cook UK Limited, p22; www.totseat.com, p36.

SECTION 1

MARKETING

Market research

In Unit 1 you learned that market research is what companies do to find out customer opinions and actions. In business, 'market' does not mean a collection of street stalls selling fruit and veg. Here, market refers to all the people who buy, or who might be persuaded to buy, a particular sort of product or service. For example:

● the market for disposable nappies is all the parents of young babies
● the market for mobile phones is most of the teenage and adult population
● the market for cycle helmets is people who ride bikes (and/or their mothers).

Market research involves each company getting the information it needs about its own particular market. The company might want to know:

● How many people are in the market for my new breakfast cereal?
● How much would they be willing to pay?
● How often would they buy?
● Does the packaging give the right image for the brand?

Market research can be **primary**, where customers or potential customers are asked directly for their opinions or shopping habits in questionnaries or group discussions, or **secondary**, when the company uses or buys research that has already been carried out by someone else, e.g. government statistics or a Mintel report.

How does a business use market research?

In 2005, after years of sales growth, Walkers suffered from a decline in sales of their crisps. Market research quickly showed that the problem was for the market as a whole – Walkers' market share was unchanged. Further research showed that the explanation was customers' increasing concern about health.

Walkers' executives decided that the only solution was to take a huge initiative – and thereby make customers see Walkers as the company at the forefront of health concerns. They would come up with a new recipe to cut the amount of saturated fat in their crisps by 80 per cent. This was done in 2006, and Gary Lineker fronted a new advertising campaign emphasising health. In 2007 Walkers' sales were growing again. Helped by market research, the company had identified the problem and the solution.

What is market research?

Primary	Explanation	Advantage	Disadvantage
Questionnaire	A business will carry out a questionnaire assessing potential demand for a product/service.	A firm can identify its target customers (age, job, etc.) – this can help with promotion and also establish the likely selling price and sales level.	Can be very time consuming – taking time to carry out the research is expensive and may not be helpful. Questions can be biased, giving misleading results.
Depth interview	This allows for more in-depth answers than a questionnaire and allows more open questions.	Interviews give firms an insight into customer perceptions and behaviour. This can help a firm decide on branding and advertising images.	Time consuming and expensive. The interviewer can sometimes affect the results, e.g. some interviewees may be too embarrassed to admit how much they really spend on chocolate.
Product testing	New products are tested on the public before they are launched.	Very useful to get consumer feedback prior to a product launch to establish likely demand and price customers are willing to pay – can stop a firm launching a product people don't like.	Time consuming and expensive. People will often say what the tester would like them to say rather than appear rude if they don't like the product.
Secondary			
Mintel report	The Marketing Intelligence reports are collated annually on more than 600 subjects, ranging from fast-food restaurants to fashion footwear.	The research has already been carried out so it is far quicker to gain market information without collecting the data yourself. It is much cheaper than primary research.	A report costs £600 (but commercial libraries have reference copies you can access for free). The research is about the market in general and won't have local information or have data relating to a new product that has not yet been launched.
Web research	Searches on the web can help identify competitors and allow a business to check on their prices and product range. Web searches will also be useful to source secondary data.	Cheap! Probably costs only the time it takes. Easy to carry out. Quicker than street interviewing.	There is a lot of rubbish on the web and care needs to be taken to ensure reliability and validity of information.

Market research at Chester Zoo

Chester Zoo carries out exit interviews with visitors, to establish how long they have spent at the zoo, where they have travelled from, which animals they liked best and how satisfied they were with the facilities.

Personnel at the zoo's marketing department state they can effectively advertise to people only when they know how old they are, where they come from, when they visit the zoo, their socio-economic **group**, how long they stay and whether they will come back. So the research helps in targeting the advertising effectively.

Establishing customer satisfaction allows the zoo to improve its services and encourage repeat visits.

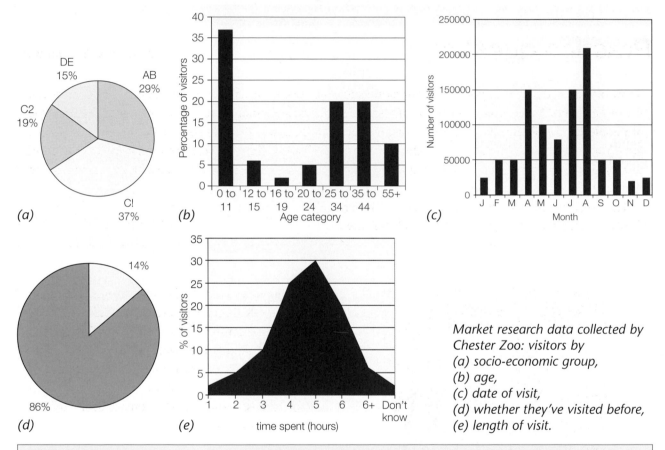

Market research data collected by Chester Zoo: visitors by
(a) socio-economic group,
(b) age,
(c) date of visit,
(d) whether they've visited before,
(e) length of visit.

Revision essentials

Primary research: when a firm carries out first-hand research by field work, e.g. a questionnaire about consumer perceptions of its products. This is usually more useful than secondary because it is 'tailor-made' to the firm's requirements.

Qualitative research: This is in-depth research using the depth interview. It is used to find consumers' behaviour and attitudes.

Quantitative research: This deals with large quantities of data, e.g. a sample size of 500 for a survey. This allows statistical analysis of the results.

Secondary research (or desk research): information from 'second-hand sources'. It could be survey results carried out by another firm, government statistics, books, websites, etc. It is much cheaper than primary research but may not meet the firm's needs.

Socio-economic group: the customers' social class. For example, people in the AB group are professionals and managers.

Exercises

Read the unit, then ask yourself:

1 Which months are the busiest at Chester Zoo? (1)
2 Why do you think these months are busiest? (4)
3 How can Chester Zoo increase visitor numbers during winter months? (6)
4 Why do you think such low numbers of teenagers visit the zoo? (4)
5 How can the zoo increase teenage visitor numbers? (6)
6 Why will knowing a visitor's socio-economic group help the zoo plan its marketing campaign? (4)

Practice questions

(20 marks; 25 minutes)

'How often, on average, do you send your clothes to the dry cleaners?' was a question asked of a sample of people for a Mintel report about trends in laundry. (There are Mintel reports about almost everything.) Of those interviewed, 48 per cent never take their clothes to the dry cleaners.

The report claims that changing consumer lifestyles mean the dry cleaning market will stagnate.

Factors such as home dry cleaning kits, improved fabric technology allowing more items to be machine washed and the increase in the number of people who work from home (who obviously don't need to wear dry clean-only suits) have all had an impact on the market.

According to a recent Mintel report, more shoes are sold in the UK than anywhere else in Europe – since 2001 spending on shoes has increased by 38 per cent. In fact, one in ten British women owns over 30 pairs of shoes, while 20 per cent own between 16 and 30 pairs (Mintel 2006). In 2006 we spent over £6.5 billion on shoes. However, the Italians still buy the most shoes (£9.8 billion).

Questions

1 Your friend is considering buying a dry cleaning business. Explain to your friend whether you consider this to be a good idea or not. (8)
2 a The research above was carried out by Mintel. What are the drawbacks of this kind of research? (4)
  b This research looks very positive, but what further research would you carry out before deciding whether to open a shoe shop in your home town? (4)
  c Why? (4)

2 Product trial and repeat purchase

Have you ever seen an advert for something on the TV, thought to yourself 'that looks great', rushed out and bought the product and been really disappointed? You have bought it once but never again.

All businesses try to persuade us that their product is the best there is. Have you seen the advertisement for **Cillit Bang**? Wouldn't you be disappointed if you bought a bottle only to discover that bang, and the dirt wasn't gone? Cillit Bang claims to be the most powerful cleaning product available on the market. If it fails to live up to that claim then people are not going to buy another bottle – they will go back to their previous brand.

Having come up with a new product, there are three things that must be got right:

- achieving distribution (getting shops to stock the product, see 'Marketing mix', Unit 6)
- **product trial** (getting people to buy it for the first time)
- **repeat purchase** (moving customers on from trial to buying regularly).

Achieving product trial

It can be hard to get people to try a new product. Not always, of course – for example, people who buy chocolate bars, canned drinks and magazines are quite willing to 'risk' their 50p or £1.50 on trying a new product. But most markets are not like this. Adults are very reluctant to 'risk' £12 on a new brand of whisky that they may not like and may hang around on a shelf for months or years. When the first Xbox came out, people who had grown up with PlayStation were reluctant to buy the newcomer.

Getting people to buy a product for the first time can be hard when:

- buyers are locked into existing brand loyalties, such as always buying Heinz beans, Gold Blend coffee, or Marmite
- buyers are locked in by earlier decisions (it's too expensive for them

to switch), e.g. PlayStation games, Microsoft Office, or someone who is halfway through a mobile phone contract
■ your new business has not yet established a reputation/brand image, so there is no reason for people to risk their money with you.

To overcome resistance to product trial is very difficult. Either it must be achieved by huge advertising spending, building up a clear brand image and persuading people that 'it must be good', or product trial must be started on a small scale, steadily building up sales by recommendation and word of mouth. **Haagen-Dazs** ice cream began in Britain with distribution in small shops, plus free samples given out at places like Wimbledon and Glastonbury. This built a network of customers who asked friends, 'Have you tried Haagen-Dazs yet?'

Repeat purchase

Repeat purchase by consumers is vital to a business's success. Launching a new product is far too expensive to make a profit if people buy once but never again. To achieve high repeat purchase (that is, **brand loyalty**), certain factors are crucial:

■ The product/service must be at least as good as the customer expected – preferably much, much better. Adults may have been buying *The Sun* for 20 years; it would take a fantastic new newspaper to get them to switch permanently away from 'their paper'.
■ The brand image must match the customer's image of him or herself. Lots of people have tried **Yakult**, but not many feel that its quirky image is what they feel about themselves; people identify far better with **Actimel's** fun, family image.
■ The product must seem value for money, either because it is cheap for what you get (*The Sun*) or because it gives you exactly what you want/need (the *Financial Times* newspaper for business people).

Once a product has become established as a reliable brand, managers can look to expand their product range and know that they have loyal customers who would be willing to try something new. For example, most of us trust **Cadbury's** chocolate and are happy to try any of its new products. From the company's point of view, this is an extra type of repeat purchase.

The **Marmite** advertising campaign 'You'll either love it or hate it' was born out of talking to people and discovering that most of them really either love or hate Marmite! This was a bold move for the brand; it brings to life the effect of the spread on different people. Marmite was telling its customers: try it and if you don't like it, don't try it again. It effectively challenged consumers to try the brand with a hope that when they tried it, they would love it, and if they didn't that was OK because some people don't.

'You can get everyone in the world to try your product once, but if the experience is less than satisfactory, the likelihood of a repeat purchase would be as thirst quenching as sand'

Joseph Jaffe, marketing speaker/author

Customer loyalty

It is important for a business to encourage consumers to stay loyal to their brands. Large manufacturers **Kellogg's**, **Adidas** and **Microsoft** are all household names which we associate with quality. As a result, we are likely to buy one of their products when we go shopping rather than an untried or unknown one. However, if any of these brands launched a product that we did not like or was of poor quality, it might cause damage to their whole business.

Revision essentials

Product trial: consumer samples a product for the first time.

Repeat purchase: consumer regularly purchases brand.

Brand loyalty: a strongly motivated and long-standing decision to purchase a particular product or service.

Exercises

(20 marks; 20 minutes)

Read the unit, then ask yourself:

1 Explain what is meant by product trial and repeat purchase. (4)

2 Outline the importance of repeat purchase to a business. (2)

3 Describe why businesses try to encourage customer loyalty. (4)

4 Explain Unilever's decision to use the 'love it or hate it' advertising campaign for Marmite. (4)

5 Identify and explain three methods that businesses can use to encourage customers to repeat purchase. (6)

Practice questions

Double Whopper, fries, Coke – oh, and a measuring tape, please.' The Advertising Standards Authority (ASA) has upheld a complaint against Burger King that a junk food portion was too small.

In comparison with the tall tower of meat, lettuce, tomato and bun featured in a recent television advertisement for the fast food franchise, investigators discovered that an actual store-bought Double Whopper burger came up short.

It is said that the camera puts on several pounds, but the ASA insisted the advert could not be re-broadcast until the size of the burger was reduced to correspond more closely to the product.

The investigation into the relative size of the Double Whopper was triggered by three complaints from consumers who believed the burger was smaller and less substantial than the product featured in a TV advert.

To check the chain's products, two ASA investigators purchased two Double Whoppers at separate London restaurants. After careful examination, they concluded that the burgers were smaller and thinner than those in the advert.

The conclusion drawn by these culinary detectives was that the advert did indeed give a 'misleading impression' of the size of the Double Whopper burger.

Source: The Scotsman, 17 January 2007

Questions

1 To what extent do you believe the Burger King brand will have been damaged after the complaint to the Advertising Standards Authority? (5)

2 Discuss what actions Burger King should now take to keep its existing customers following the complaint against it being upheld. (5)

3 Briefly explain how the news of this embarrassment for Burger King might affect a) product trial and b) repeat purchase of the Double Whopper. (8)

4 If you were invited to invest in a Burger King restaurant at this stage, what changes would you insist on beforehand? Explain your reasoning. (7)

3   Product life cycle

When deciding on its marketing strategy, a firm will have to examine the existing position of its products and services. Only by looking at how its products are doing will it be able to decide what to do next. One technique a firm can use to do this is the product life cycle.

All new products have an expected life cycle. A product's life cycle is the number of weeks or years a business expects the product to sell. There are four stages in the product life cycle. These give an idea of where the product is in its lifetime – a bit like a human life.

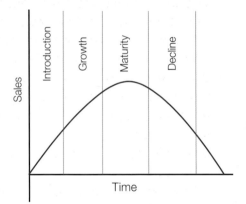

The product life cycle

Stage 1: Introduction

First the company spends a lot of time and money researching the product and the market for the product. The product will be tested and market research carried out before it is launched. There will be no sales at this time. The business will be preparing an advertising campaign. At this stage costs are high and there are no sales. The product is then launched and placed on the market. There will be low product sales and small-scale distribution. Any advertising will be informative to make people aware that the product exists. The product might be the only one of its kind at this stage so the selling price will probably be high. At this stage sales are low and costs are high.

Stage 2: Growth

At this stage the product becomes known in the market and there will be a wider distribution network. The business will continue with advertising but it will be less frequent than at the product's launch. At this stage customer awareness increases, the price will still be high and sales and profits start to rise.

Stage 3: Maturity

The market may become saturated as 'me-too' or copycat products are launched onto the market. Sales growth flattens out and cash flow improves. Advertising is persuasive and is used to remind the market that the product exists. The business may try to increase promotion in an attempt to maintain market share – money spent on reinforcing the brand image or packaging. Profits are still good. The product is in a highly competitive market and weak brands often disappear at this stage, as they cannot compete.

Stage 4: Decline

The product's sales and profits start to fall. The product is no longer offering what customers want or new technology used by other products has made it out of date. Some businesses will stop their marketing to cut costs but will still make some profits between now and when the product is finally withdrawn. Eventually the product is taken out of production. The last products are often sold at a reduced price, meaning a further reduction in profits. The product is withdrawn from the market.

In reality very few products follow the cycle exactly. The length of each stage will vary a lot. Businesses can take actions to prolong a stage, such as heavy brand advertising to try to stop maturity turning into decline. Not all products go through each stage – some go straight from introduction to decline (think of Chico from *The X Factor!*). It is important for businesses to know what stage of the life cycle their products are at so that they can plan the correct marketing strategy for the product.

Just because a product has reached the maturity stage or even started decline does not necessarily mean it is the end. Some products will have **extension strategies** launched for them to start to increase sales again, for example by changing the product's design or use.

> *Marketing is not an event, but a process … It has a beginning, a middle, but never an end, for it is a process. You improve it, perfect it, change it, even pause it. But you never stop it completely.*
> Jay Conrad Levinson, author on marketing

Extension strategies

Firms may try to prevent sales going into decline by using extension strategies. There are various techniques they can use:

- **Find new uses for the product**. **Johnson's** Baby Powder was originally marketed only for babies; realising its sales potential among women was a major breakthrough for the company.
- **Develop a wider product range.** **Fairy** washing-up liquid, Fairy Power Spray, Fairy dishwasher powder/tablets.

- **Change the appearance, format or packaging.** Coke cans, bottles, etc.
- **Encourage use of the product on more occasions** – e.g. shampoo, wash hair twice; cereals, not just for breakfast; ice cream in the winter.
- **Adapt the product**. 'New and improved.'
- **Reduce the price** – e.g. when the product moves from being newly introduced to an everyday item.

Cash flow and the life cycle

Cash flow is the term used for the money going in and out of the business. Cash flow is affected by the different stages of the product life cycle.

At the start of the cycle there is no cash flow inflow as money is paid out to design, develop and launch the product. Cash flow then improves until the product reaches the end of growth. By the time the product moves into maturity, cash flow is positive. This remains the case until the product starts to go into decline, when cash flow will become negative again unless the business introduces an extension strategy.

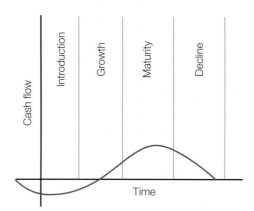

Cash flow over the product life cycle

Businesses try to have a range of products at different stages of their life cycles so that all the products do not reach the decline stage at the same time. They try to make sure that there are always some products at the mature stage and some in the introductory and growth stages in order to ensure that they have a positive cash flow and are making a profit.

Revision essentials

Extension strategy: an attempt to prolong the sales of a product and prevent it from declining.

Exercises

Read the unit, then ask yourself:

1 Describe what happens during the introduction stage of a product's life. (2)

2 Outline what could happen to profits for a product which is at the maturity stage. (2)

3 Explain why some products have much longer life cycles than others. Use examples to illustrate your answer. (4)

4 Look at the examples below and match up the statement to the life cycle. (4)

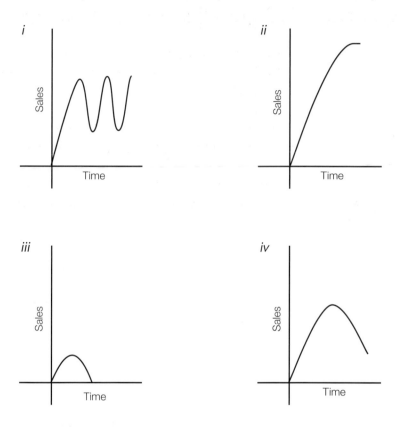

a A product which is very popular but which after a time loses its popularity.

b A new product which flops.

c A product which becomes popular very quickly and continues to have good sales.

d A product for which sales vary, season by season.

5 Think of examples of real products that would match up with the product life cycle descriptions in the previous question. (4)

6 Draw a product life cycle for a car such as the Volkswagen Golf and then describe the stages and explain what is happening to cash flow at each stage. (9)

Practice questions

(25 marks; 30 minutes)

When Cadbury Dairy Milk chocolate was introduced in the early 1900s it made an immediate impact, quickly becoming the market leader. The success story has continued. It is still the top-selling chocolate brand in the UK and the Cadbury mega brand's broad family of products today has an international retail value approaching US$1 billion.

As an international brand Cadbury Dairy Milk carries the same distinctive image all over the world. Wherever you buy a bar of Cadbury Dairy Milk the pack design will be exactly the same, only the language will be different.

The famous slogan 'glass and a half of full cream milk in every half pound' with the picture of milk pouring into the chocolate bar is one of the all-time greats of British advertising.

The first two additions to the Cadbury mega brand family were Fruit & Nut in 1928 and WholeNut in 1933. The family has since been extended and there are now ten varieties of Cadbury Dairy Milk bars in the range.

(*Source: www.cadbury.co.uk*)

Questions

1 Outline what you think has made Cadbury Dairy Milk so successful. (3)

2 Draw a product life cycle for Cadbury Dairy Milk and describe what is happening at each stage. (6)

3 Explain why Cadbury might have decided to extend the Dairy Milk brand. (4)

4 Identify other strategies that Cadbury might have used. (4)

5 Describe how the product life cycle might help Cadbury in its marketing planning. (4)

6 Outline two possible extension strategies Cadbury could use if sales of Dairy Milk started to decline. (4)

4 The Boston Matrix

Product portfolio analysis

Most businesses do not rely on selling just one product; they have a range of products that they sell. This is called their product portfolio. All these products will vary in their popularity. Firms such as **L'Oreal** have many different products and brands. The managers need to decide which of these to concentrate most of their effort on. A tool that can be used by a business to compare their products and to work out how they are doing is the Boston Matrix.

The Boston Matrix

The Boston Matrix allows businesses to measure the extent to which an individual product is succeeding within its market. It looks at the success of a brand in terms of its market share and market growth.

Businesses need a variety of products to be available at any one time to ensure that they are not only making profits today but also have good profit prospects tomorrow.

The Boston Matrix helps decision-making using portfolio analysis. The analysis looks at the position of these products or services in their

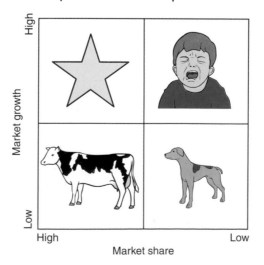

relevant markets. The Boston Matrix looks at the market share and growth in the area in which a business operates. There are four categories within the Boston Matrix: Rising Star, Problem Child, Cash Cow and Dog. A business would look at each individual product in its range (or portfolio) and place it onto the matrix. It would do this for every product in the range.

Problem Children are products that have low market share in a high-growth market. They need lots of money spent on them if they are going to become stars. They are frustrating because they have so much potential yet aren't successful. Should the company try to turn them into stars? Or accept that they are flops? **Nestlé's** water brand Perrier is in that position.

Rising Stars are products with high market share in a high-growth market. They generate lots of sales but often need lots of money to be spent on them as the market is growing as well. Stars tend to generate high amounts of income. Businesses should keep and build their stars. Stars are destined to become the Cash Cows of the future.

Cash Cows are products with high market share in a low-growth market. They generate lots of sales and huge profits. Examples include **Coca-Cola** and **Persil** detergent. Profits from these products are used to help fund Problem Children or Stars. Cash Cows generate more than is invested in them. They are best kept in a portfolio of products for the time being.

Dogs are products with low market share and low growth. They may have been Cash Cows or Problem Children before they moved into the Dog category. Businesses want as few Dogs as possible because they add little to the portfolio. Sometimes a business retains Dogs because they still make some low sales, which may attract customers to buy other products from the business. They have no real future, so as soon as they stop generating cash they are 'put to sleep'.

Working with the Boston Matrix

Sony BMG Music Entertainment is a global recorded music joint venture with a roster of current artists that includes a broad array of both local artists and international superstars. The artists signed to Sony

'*The toughest thing about success is that you've got to keep on being a success.*'
Irving Berlin

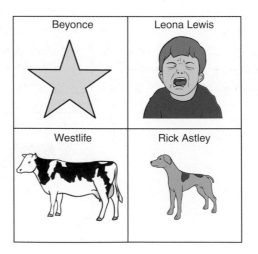

BMG include Beyonce, Leona Lewis, Rick Astley and Westlife, among many others (source: **www.sonybmg.co.uk**).

We can use the Boston Matrix to analyse the 'products' of Sony BMG (see figure). Sony BMG can look at the artists and where they are positioned on the matrix to make some decisions.

Leona Lewis won the 2006 series of *The X Factor.* She is going to have to have a lot of money invested in her if she is going to become a star. Money will be spent on marketing and styling. Sony BMG has to make sure it finds the right songs for her to sing or she could become a Dog.

Beyonce is a very popular artist. But she still needs a lot of marketing as she is in a highly competitive market, with lots of similar artists. So while she may be the best in this genre at the moment, Sony BMG has to spend money to make sure she stays there.

Westlife generate a lot of sales. When they release a single, it goes to number one. There are plenty of Westlife fans who have supported the band for years. Westlife do not need lots of marketing and promotion, their fans love them!

Rick Astley was a big star in the 1980s. Then, he would have been positioned as a Star on the matrix, but the market changed and he is now more of a Dog. However, there has been an 80s revival in recent years, which is perhaps why Sony BMG still has him signed to its label.

Problems with the matrix

Businesses often assume that they will make more profit if the market share is high, but this might not always be the case. When **Airbus** launched the new A380 plane, it may have gained a high market share quickly but the extremely high costs of development still have to be covered.

Sometimes things can be over-simplified. A product may be a Dog, but sales might pick up. **Heinz** announced it was to stop making salad cream a few years ago, but sales recovered and it is now a Cash Cow once again.

Revision essentials

Boston Matrix: a tool that can compare the products of a business and work out how they are doing.

Stars: products that are in high-growth markets with a relatively high share of that market.

Problem Children: products with a low share of a high-growth market.

Cash Cows: Products with a high share of a slow-growth market.

Dogs: products with a low share of a low-growth market.

Exercises

Read the unit, then ask yourself:

1 What is meant by the Boston Matrix? (3)

2 Describe the benefits to a business of using the Boston Matrix to help make business decisions. (6)

3 Identify two limitations to a business of using the Boston Matrix. (2)

4 **a** Complete a portfolio analysis for a manufacturer that you know well, such as Kellogg's, Cadbury or Nike. Consider how their brands fit into the Boston Matrix categories. (6)

   b Discuss whether the firm seems to be managing its product portfolio effectively. (8)

Practice questions

Unilever has been trading for more than a century. Its website says that its aim is to meet people's everyday needs for nutrition, home hygiene and personal care. It does this with brands that help people 'feel good, look good and get more out of life'.

Sixteen out of forty brands are market leaders, including Persil, Dove, Magnum, Flora, Marmite and Lynx. You can find Unilever products in the kitchens, fridges, freezers and bathrooms of nine out of every ten UK homes. Unilever has annual UK sales of nearly 2.5 billion.

One important category of brands is 'home hygiene'. The brands are Cif, Comfort, Domestos, Persil, Persil Washing Up Liquid and Surf. Within these brands there are liquid, tablet and gel forms of the products.

Questions

1 Explain one possible reason why Unilever produces such a vast range of products. (3)

2 **a** Use your judgement to complete a product portfolio analysis of Unilever's home hygiene range. (5)

   b Justify the choices you have made. (4)

3 Discuss the importance to a company such as Unilever of having so many market leaders within its portfolio. (8)

5 Branding and differentiation

Have you heard of **Apple**? Do you know what it makes? What does the name mean to you? Does it mean quality? Does it mean expensive?

Apple manufactures a range of products, from iMacs to iPods to iTunes. We see the Apple logo and we instantly recognise and know what it means. How do we know this? Apple has created a **brand**; it has bombarded consumers with advertising and promotion that have made us remember its logo. We are convinced about the quality of the company's products and image. Existing customers trust a strong brand such as Apple as they know what to expect. The **logo** on a product is an important part of the product.

Branding gives an identity to a product. Producers hope that consumers will become loyal to their brand and always buy their product rather than any other. Every business wants to be a customer's first choice. Building and managing a brand can play a significant part in making that happen. Brands give potential customers a firm idea of what they're buying before they buy it, making the purchasing decision easier.

A brand can be the name of a product, such as Dairy Milk, or it can be the name of a company that markets a number of products under its brand name, Virgin for example.

Branding is establishing an identity for your product that distinguishes it from the competition. Brands aren't just for big companies – they can make smaller businesses stand out from the crowd, particularly in competitive markets. Successful branding adds value to an item and can ensure brand loyalty. Brand loyalty exists when consumers buy your product on a regular basis.

> 'Products are made in the factory, but brands are created in the mind.'
> Walter Landor, German designer

Types of branding

- **Family branding**: products are distinguished under a company heading. Apple's product mix consists of iMac, MacPro, Mac Mini, Apple TV, iPod, iTunes. All the products are distinguished under the Apple banner.

- **Line branding**: products are distinguished from other producers' products, e.g. Wrigleys Extra, Extra Thin Ice, Juicy Fruit, Hubba Bubba, Airwaves, Orbit Spearmint and Doublemint.

Some retailers use 'own-label' brands, where they use their name of the product rather than the manufacturers', like **Sainsbury's** 'Taste The Difference' range of food. These tend to be cheaper than the normal brands, but usually give the retailer more profit than selling an advertised brand.

Some brands are so strong that they have become global brands. This means that the product is sold in lots of countries all over the world and the contents are very similar. Examples of global brands include Apple, Coca-Cola, Warner Bros., BMW and Lexmark.

The advantages of having a strong brand are:

- it encourages customer loyalty, leading to repeat purchases and word-of-mouth recommendation
- companies are able to charge higher prices, especially if the brand is the market leader
- retailers want to stock top-selling brands. With limited shelf space it is more likely the top brands will be on the shelf ahead of less well-known brands.

The disadvantages of branding are:

- there are high costs associated with promotion in order to gain brand recognition in the first place
- constant promotion is necessary to maintain the brand
- a single bad event may affect all the brand's products
- brand names have to be protected by being registered worldwide.

All companies try to make their products different to those of their rivals, even if only in some tiny or cosmetic way. They attempt to differentiate their products, in other words to make customers believe the product is really special. A strong brand name helps hugely in this process.

> 'A product can be copied by a competitor; a brand is unique. A product can be quickly outdated; a successful brand is timeless.'
> Stephen King, WPP Group, London

Product differentiation

Product **differentiation** makes customers feel there is a good range of products to choose from. But it can lead to higher prices for consumers. For example, in the market for sweets there are many different types of mint: Tic Tacs, Softmints, Extra Strong Mints, Polos and so on. All are made from sugar plus mint essence, i.e. they are the same. But the differentiation is clear, with different strengths of mint, types of packaging, hardness/chewiness and so on.

There are several other ways in which businesses can differentiate their product or service from the competition:

- logo
- name

- quality
- content
- packaging
- design.

A product has a **unique selling point (USP)** when it has an important feature that other products do not have. For example, Bounty's USP is that it is the only widely sold chocolate bar with a coconut filling. Having a USP is the ultimate form of product differentiation.

Revision essentials

Logo: a symbol or picture that represents the business.

Brand: a product with a unique character, for instance in design or image.

Differentiation: the process of making a product seem distinct from its competitors.

Unique selling point (USP): a key feature of a product that is not shared by any of its rivals.

Exercises

(35 marks; 35 minutes)

Read the unit, then ask yourself:

1 Explain in your own words what is meant by branding. (2)

2 Think of a brand you know. Identify what type of branding the manufacturers have used. (2)

3 Describe what a business must do to turn a product into a brand. (3)

4 Outline **two** benefits to a business of creating a brand. (4)

5 Identify the advantages and drawbacks to a small business of creating and maintaining a brand. (6)

6 Explain why a business would want to differentiate its products from those of its nearest rivals. (4)

7 There are many brands of cola, each of which is fairly well differentiated. Identify how the different brands on the market have been differentiated. (3)

8 Discuss whether there are real differences in the products or whether it is all just image and reputation. (5)

9 Which do you think is the number one brand in the UK today for the following products:
   a MP3 players
   b Trainers
   c Breakfast cereals
   d Dog food
   e Jeans
   f Toothpaste. (6)

Practice questions

What's the first thing that springs to mind when the brand 'Club 18–30' is mentioned? Whatever it is, that is the purpose of a brand – to create an identity with a product or service that draws people to that product or service over those of a rival.

The Club 18–30 brand is owned by Thomas Cook. It has decided to try to 'change the perception' of the brand but not, it claims, change the image. The perception of a brand is how people see it; the image is what the brand reflects, what it wants to be associated with.

Thomas Cook is planning to introduce new activities on its Club 18–30 holidays, including scuba diving, paint-balling and golf. It believes that it has to respond to a changing market and suggests that the youth market at which it is aiming is becoming more sophisticated in what it wants from a holiday. It has employed an advertising agency to spearhead a £1.5 million marketing campaign starting in February and plans to boost sales by 10 per cent during 2005.

Club 18–30 has been at the centre of a number of unfavourable news items in recent years. Incidents have involved Club 18–30 staff who have caused offence in Greece where Faliraki has become the centre of the 'yob culture', according to papers like *The Sun*.

It now seems that Faliraki has become yesterday's resort and that new venues are being sought as the fun centres for holidays for the young. Club 18–30, it seems, is trying to reflect that changing market. This is not the first time Club 18–30 has tried to change its image. In 2004 it announced it was not encouraging bar crawls and wet T-shirt competitions and also dropped Benidorm from its list of resorts as it was becoming too much like 'Blackpool on the Med' and not the sort of thing its more sophisticated market segment wanted out of a holiday.

Source:
www.bized.ac.uk

Questions

1 Explain what is meant by the term 'brand'. (2)
2 Describe how Thomas Cook has differentiated Club 18–30 from other packaged holiday firms. (4)
3 Explain why Thomas Cook might have chosen to differentiate Club 18–30 in the way that it did. (6)
4 Outline why Thomas Cook might want to change the brand image of Club 18–30. (4)
5 Describe the process Thomas Cook will have to go through in order to recreate the brand for Club 18–30. (4)

6 Building a successful marketing mix

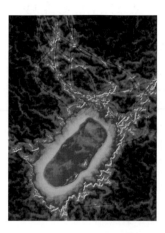

In 2006 more than 1 million of bars of **Cadbury's** chocolate had to be recalled and destroyed. The company had found traces of salmonella (a nasty stomach bug) in one of its factories. Putting this right cost Cadbury more than £30 million. Despite this embarrassment, however, 2006 provided the company with one success – the launch of the Cadbury's Creme Egg bar.

Given that one in six new products fails, how did Cadbury succeed despite the salmonella scandal? It could be argued that this is down to successful marketing.

The **marketing mix** is made up of four elements – product, price, promotion and place. In order to be successful a firm must make sure it has:

- the right product/service (that customers like and want to buy)
- at the right price (communicating the right **image** – not so low as to seem 'cheap', nor too high not to seem value for money)
- promoted using the right medium (TV, radio, magazines, newspapers, special offers)
- is available in the right place (**Chanel** at Selfridges; **Lynx** at Superdrug).

Product

The easiest route to sales success is to have a great product. Years ago, people believed that all you needed to do was to 'build a better mousetrap' and sales would flow. In other words, make the best product and you will get the highest sales. This is less true today, when no one is sure what is 'the best' product. One year people are eating low-calorie yoghurts, the next they are told that Omega-3 yoghurts are better.

Well-run firms try hard to keep in close touch with customers to find out what they want. Then they can provide the right product (or service) to match the customers' needs. Examples of great products include:

- the Lexus 430: the ultimate smooth saloon car – the Japanese car that conquered America
- Cadbury's Creme Egg: just hits that pre-Easter spot
- *The Sun:* the first newspaper to realise that most people prefer their news to be fun rather than serious
- Primark: realising the opportunity for up-to-date but affordable fashion.

Price

The key is to ensure that the price is 'right'. In some cases this may be very expensive. A **Lexus** 430 costs £55,000; it will never outsell the Ford Focus, but Lexus customers wouldn't want everyone to have one! At £55,000, though, Lexus customers are able to convince themselves that they are getting value for money.

Broadly, there are two different types of product/service: price-makers and price-takers. Price-makers have, like Lexus, such a strong brand name and such a good product that they can set their own price. Others may follow. In the case of a price-taker, the producer is a follower. The *Daily Express* follows the price lead set by the *Daily Mail;* British Airways' European flight prices follow the lead set by Ryanair.

Strong brands are price leaders; weaker ones are price-takers.

Promotion

In this case, promotion means all the ways companies can use to persuade customers to buy. These include advertising, which may be used as a way of building a strong brand identity in the long term ('L'Oreal, because I'm worth it'). There are also many ways of trying to boost short-term sales, such as sales promotions: Buy One Get One Free (BOGOF), enter a competition, introductory prices and so on.

The key to successful promotion is that it should not only build sales but also build the brand image. Tactics such as BOGOFs can cheapen the image of a brand.

Place

This element of the marketing mix is about how to get the product from the producer to the customer. The easiest way, today, is to sell directly, via the internet. Many people love to go shopping, though, so retail sales remain very important. There are three main distribution channels:

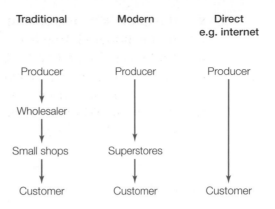

Traditional	Modern	Direct e.g. internet
Producer	Producer	Producer
↓		
Wholesaler		
↓	↓	↓
Small shops	Superstores	
↓	↓	
Customer	Customer	Customer

In addition to choosing the most appropriate channel, firms must decide the type of store they wish to be distributed in. Posh crisp maker **Tyrrells** decided it would rather not have its products on sale in Tesco. The directors believed the image of the brand would be built more successfully by being seen in small shops, plus the more upmarket retailers such as Waitrose and Booths.

Why do some products fail?

Launching new products is difficult in all markets because customers get used to the papers they read, the soaps they watch and the chocolate they munch. Most markets are so crowded that it is very hard to find room for a new product success. This is clear when you read this insight into a 2007 new product launch.

There are 30 women's weekly magazines in the UK market. Yet 5 February 2007 saw the launch of another weekly – *Look* magazine. The front cover of the preview issue featured pictures of Posh Beckham, Kate Moss, Lindsay Lohan and Angelina Jolie, plus there was an insert shouting 'Just In At Primark!' Nothing new here, then.

Fewer than one in eight new magazines becomes successful – will *Look* be lucky?

Owners IPC magazines invested £18 million in 18 months of planning for the launch and hired a massive editorial staff of 40. The sales target for *Look* was to sell 250,000 copies a week within 12 months. This seemed an ambitious target, as *Grazia* magazine was already filling a similar niche (for a glossy, fashion-orientated weekly) but selling only 175,000 copies.

Editor Ali Hall targeted *Look* at 24-year-old women, keen on celebrities, even keener on shopping, and with a Saturday High Street ritual of Topshop, H&M, Primark and Dorothy Perkins. Hall thinks this is distinctly different from *Grazia,* which, she says, is for 30-year-olds who are into brands such as Burberry and Chloe. *Look* is about youth, celebrities and style – not brands.

At the heart of the product is the promise that *Look* will give readers the quickest insights into what's hot and what's not. Sections will include 'High Street's Hottest' and 'High Street Spy'. The latter will track down what celebs are wearing and where to buy it (or buy the High Street imitation).

For £9 million of marketing spend, IPC is launching a huge promotional programme, giving away 1.2 million copies at supermarkets plus shopping malls such as Bluewater and the Trafford Centre. There will also be a big launch TV campaign.

A key decision has been over pricing. Unlike celeb magazines such as *Heat* and *OK!, Look* is produced on high-quality gloss paper. It will look as good as rival *Grazia* and monthlies such as *Marie Claire.* Despite the expensive gloss paper, *Look* is to be priced at £1.30, significantly below Grazia's £1.80.

The *Look* marketing mix

PRODUCT	PRICE
Glossy, high production values, expensive-to-produce magazine. Targeting 24-year-old women with a sharp eye on fashion and celebrities	£1.30 launch price compared with *Grazia* at £1.80. Other top-selling weeklies include: *OK!*: £2.00 *Hello*: £1.85 *Heat*: £1.65 *Now*: £1.10
PROMOTION	PLACE
TV advertising plus a huge programme of giveaways for the launch issue (1.2 million copies to be given away). This is known as sampling and selling	Standard distribution through newsagents, supermarkets and sweet shops. *Look* will easily get distribution in WH Smith (though will have to pay to get good display positions, e.g. by the cash desks)

What does a successful marketing mix look like?

According to statistics from ALVA (Association of Leading Visitor Attractions), **Blackpool Pleasure Beach** was the leading visitor attraction for 2004 and 2005, drawing 2 million more visitors than the British Museum and 5 million more visitors than Chester Zoo. In 2006 came the news that nearby rival Southport Pleasureland was closing. So what makes Blackpool Pleasure Beach so successful?

The Blackpool Pleasure Beach marketing mix

PRODUCT	PRICE
A theme park with rides for all ages, e.g. bumper cars, soft play areas and white-knuckle rides. Home of the biggest roller coaster in the world (The Big One). It also houses bingo halls and arcade games, plus a circus and shows including ice dance. The park offers a range of refreshments in restaurants and bars. It has themed areas, e.g. Wild West, and offers visitors souvenirs and the chance to buy photos of themselves on rides	Visitors are charged for the rides they use and can therefore budget; visitors are not penalised for waiting times. They do have pre-paid wristbands available. It is a cheaper day out than competitors such as Alton Towers and provides out-of-season special offers. More popular rides are more expensive and there are cheaper rides for younger visitors. Visitors can leave the park and come back later in the day

PROMOTION	PLACE
The park is well known and has a good reputation (word of mouth). It uses a variety of promotion methods, including TV advertisements, the internet, special offers, regional newspapers, free news coverage for charity events and the illuminations and when celebrities visit (e.g. Robbie Williams who rode The Big One). The park puts leaflets in other local attractions and gives special offers through local accommodation providers	Close to large populations of Manchester and Liverpool and to other attractions in Blackpool. It provides onsite parking. Blackpool is a year-round resort with visitors to the beach during the summer, the illuminations in the autumn and Christmas breaks. There is no competition within Blackpool and Southport Pleasureland closed in 2006. There are many hotels nearby (though Blackpool really wants a big casino).

Revision essentials

Marketing mix: how a business persuades customers to buy its products/services. It is focused upon having the right product/service that customers want/need, available at a price they are willing to pay, in a place they are willing to travel to and promoted in a way to appeal to them.

Image: how a business is perceived by the general public, e.g. most people believe the Co-op to be an ethical business due not only to its business practices but also to the way it markets itself.

Exercises

(25 marks; 30 minutes)

Read the unit, then ask yourself:

1 At its launch, explain whether Look appears to be a price-maker or a price-taker. (4)

2 Do you think *Look's* marketing mix was likely to lead to a successful product launch? Explain your reasoning. (8)

3 Choose one of the following products and outline what you believe to be its marketing mix: Sony PS3, Specsavers, Pampers, Maltesers (8)

4 Looking at the marketing mix for Blackpool Pleasure Beach and explain what you think makes it successful. (5)

Practice questions

Sony launches Photo Go software

Sony has launched new software that allows users to edit and share photos and promises to be 'a fun, fast and easy way to organise, edit and share digital photos'.

Photo Go software lets users import photos from a camera or computer, then, using built-in editing tools, rotate, straighten and crop photos. Users can also adjust colour, brightness and contrast, and remove red eye.

When they have finished editing, users can share their images in a slideshow, print them using their own digital photo printer, email photos to family and friends, or upload them directly to the Sony ImageStation processing site.

The new consumer photo-editing software enables quick searching for pictures using tags, titles and other keywords. Photo Go software supports all popular image formats including .jpeg, .tif, .bmp and .png.

The key features of Photo Go are:

- interactive Show Me How tutorials
- the ability to import pictures from a USB-connected camera, memory card reader or CD/DVD ROM
- search for pictures using tags, titles and other keywords
- rate favourite pictures for reference
- organise photos using customisable data labels
- group photos by year, month, day and file size
- create and view slideshows on computer
- rotate, straighten, mirror and crop photos
- adjust colour, brightness and contrast to create the perfect look
- auto-adjust photos with one click
- correct photos with red eye reduction
- email photos to family and friends
- Order prints online directly from www.image station.com.

Photo Go is available now priced £19.99 and includes a coupon for 100 free 4 × 6 prints from Sony ImageStation.

Source: *What Digital Camera*, January 2007, © *What Digital Camera* / IPC+ Syndication

Questions

1 Part of Sony's promotion includes the coupon for free photos from Sony Image Station. How else should the company promote this software? (6)
2 Why has Sony charged £19.99 instead of £20? (2)
3 The article does not tell you where you can buy the product. What would you recommend for the 'place' element of the marketing mix? Explain your answer. (6)
4 Why might this new product fail? (6)

SECTION 2

MEETING CUSTOMER NEEDS

7 Introduction to meeting customer needs

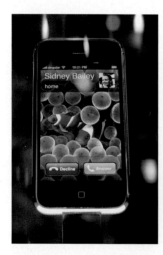

In January 2007 **Apple** announced the launch of its iPhone. Everyone had known that Apple had been working on a phone iPod, yet boss Steve Jobs managed to make the audience gasp with surprise and delight. His design team had produced such a distinctive, original product that everyone could see huge sales potential. That day, Apple shares rose by 7 per cent in the stock market, making the company worth an extra £500 million.

Apple had thought deeply about what customers would want from a single handset. The answer was a phone, a music player, a camera, text messaging and internet access – all in an attractive, convenient package. The design solution was to give it a touch screen and no buttons – and to make it look beautiful.

As he launched it, Steve Jobs said: 'The iPod changed everything in 2001. We're going to do it again in 2007 with the iPhone.'

On both occasions, Apple's skill was in anticipating customer needs and desires – then finding a way of beating **customer expectations**. Apple made the iPhone a 'must-have' item, then set a UK launch price of £300+.

Key factors in meeting customer needs

1 Keeping close to the customer. Every Friday, **Tesco** boss Terry Leahy gets out of his office and visits a couple of stores. By talking directly to shop floor staff, he is confident that he will keep in touch with ordinary shoppers. For the same reason, he will join a check-out queue and chat to a few of his customers.

Hard though he is trying, Terry Leahy cannot always get it right. After all, he is boss of a business with more than 250,000 staff, so how can he see them all?

Every week, *The Grocer* trade magazine reports on customer service among the supermarkets. Each week a different town is visited and a secret visit is made to all the main stores. Then a winner is announced: the shop of the week. The judging is based on how well each store meets customer needs. The grocery trade believes these are:

- full range of stock
- short queues at the check-out
- a clearly laid-out store
- friendly, helpful staff.

In the six months to January 2007, **Morrisons** proved the best store by far. Perhaps because of this, Morrisons had a more successful Christmas 2006 than any of its rivals. Surprisingly, despite Terry Leahy's efforts, Tesco came bottom of the list.

In other businesses, different factors will be the key to success in meeting customer needs. Table 7.1 sets out some of the possibilities.

Table 7.1

BUSINESS SITUATION	KEYS TO MEETING CUSTOMERS' NEEDS
Cafe in university student area	Cheap, with generous portions; open until late; internet access; some reference to organic or Fair Trade items.
Dentist	Minimum wait; minimum pain; minimum sense of guilt (at too many Mars Bars; too little flossing).
Buying a new Volvo car	Friendly, efficient service; reliable car that's easy – or fun – to drive; terrific sound system; petrol less punishing than expected.
Manufacturing scarves	Great designs – to meet different people's needs; different price levels: £6.99 scarves for teenagers, £14.99 scarves for middle-aged customers; making sure stock is available, especially in the autumn.
Professional football club	Three points this Saturday, no matter how poor the game, the pies and the programme.

'To all our nit-picky, over-demanding, ask-awkward-questions customers: Thank you, and keep up the good work.'

Dell computers advertisement

'You ponce in here expecting to be waited on hand and foot, well I'm trying to run a hotel here.'

Basil Fawlty, hotelkeeper, aka John Cleese, actor, *Fawlty Towers*

2 Being efficient and reliable. Customers want their needs met consistently. The trains on the London–Manchester route are smart, new and fast. This meets many customer needs. They also have a highly varied pricing policy, which lets students travel for £30 return while business people are paying £270 to be on the same train. No one will be happy, though, if the service is unreliable. Success relies on careful planning and an eye for detail. In the case of a railway or an airline, engineers should check regularly to prevent things going wrong, rather than waiting to fix things that have broken down.

3 Providing great design. Many customers value design and style above price. They want clothes that make them look great, cosmetics that make them look older – or younger – and cars that make them look successful, or exciting, or smooth. As mentioned above, it boils down to getting close to the customer. Some people will buy only the best; others want £2.99 T-shirts for some days but £24.99 tops for Friday and Saturday nights. Well-run businesses learn what customers want, then recruit people with the right skills to be able to supply them.

Exercises

(20 marks; 20 minutes)

Read the unit, then ask yourself:

1 Nokia, the world's biggest-selling producer of phones, would be worried about Apple's new iPhone. Outline two ways in which Nokia might respond to the launch of the iPhone. (6)

2 Re-read Table 7.1, then suggest the keys to meeting customers' needs for a supplier of:

   a baby car seats (4)

   b lipstick. (4)

3 Name two types of customer who might not 'value design and style above price'. (2)

4 Put in your own words what is meant by the phrase 'get close to your customer'. (4)

Practice questions

(25 marks; 25 minutes)

On 2 January 2007 Little Chef went into liquidation (it closed down). It was quickly bought for £10 million, but that was little compensation for owners Lawrence Wosskow and Simon Heath. They had paid £52 million for the business just one year before. It was also a very worrying time for Little Chef's 3500 employees – the new owners made it clear from the start that they would close at least 60 of the 235 outlets.

Staff would be especially concerned because Little Chef eateries have always been on A roads, i.e. roads going between towns or cities, and therefore often in the middle of nowhere. There would be few alternative jobs nearby.

When reporting on the collapse of the Little Chef chain, many newspapers said it was 'stuck in a time-warp'. Started up in 1958, it expanded in the 1970s and many outlets still looked the same today. Its 2007 menu of an 'Olympic Breakfast' (£6.99) and 'Gammon & Pineapple' (£7.50) was crazily far away from the modern concern for healthy eating. Even the firm's logo was a problem because outside every Little Chef was the 'Fat Charlie' symbol – looking just the way that no one wants to look today.

In the 1950s, 1960s and 1970s, Little Chef served up the big portions of greasy food people wanted. As tastes changed, the business stayed stuck with a Fat Charlie outlook and image. One reporter visited a Little Chef in Tabley, Cheshire and mentioned the cheery, quick service. Yet good service means nothing if the wrong products are being offered or the prices are too high.

Fat Charlie has had his day.

Questions

1 Outline two reasons why staff at Little Chef would be worried about the news they heard about the business in early 2007. (4)

2 A section of the text mentions the importance of friendly, helpful staff. How does the story about Little Chef show that this factor is not enough to ensure business success? (4)

3 Discuss whether Little Chef managed to stay close to its customers during recent years. (8)

4 Discuss a suitable strategy the new owners might adopt to make the most of their £10 million investment. (9)

Design and R&D

Introduction

In July 2006 the *Dragon's Den* TV programme featured a new invention. James Seddon was trying to get £75,000 of investment for his 'Eggxactly' water-free egg cooker (a kind of boiled egg sandwich toaster). James invented the product to meet a specific 'customer need'. His three-year-old daughter loved soft-boiled eggs, but James kept overcooking them. Therefore he had to throw the egg away and start again.

As a scientist, James saw that soft-polymer plastics could grip an egg and provide the contact for electric wires to heat and cook it. Electronic controls could then provide the timers and the heat controls to generate a perfect soft-boiled or hard-boiled egg (and ring a buzzer when the egg was cooked).

Scientific research such as this can provide a business with an edge over its competitors. When the research leads to the discovery of a new product, a **patent** can be registered. This provides the inventor with up to 20 years before anyone else is allowed to copy the idea. During this long period of time, the inventor has the opportunity to charge prices that are high enough to recover the costs of the original scientific work.

Although the *Dragon* investors offered James his £75,000, he later turned this down as an American investor was prepared to offer much more capital. In March 2007 James spoke confidently about launching the product in Britain and America during 2007.

> 'You can design and create and build the most wonderful place in the world. But it takes people to make the dream a reality.'
> Walt Disney

Design and the design mix

Having come up with the Eggxactly idea, James Seddon then needed to consider what the egg cooker would look like. Would it be shaped like a chicken? Or would it just be a square box, looking like a sandwich toaster?

James needed to consider the three aspects of the design mix:

1 Economic manufacture: making sure that the design allows the product to be made cost effectively; a complex design might add 50 per cent to the manufacturing cost, making the product too expensive for some customers.

2 Function: the design must make sure that the product works well and works every time. The **Sony** Bravia TV does not look any different from other flat-screen TVs, until you turn it on. Then the higher quality picture shines through. Sony invested heavily in making it function better than other TVs. In the case of the egg cooker, precise controls will be essential – to make the perfect soft-boiled egg, time after time.

3 Aesthetics: how well does the product appeal to the senses? It may work well and be inexpensive to make but look or feel cheap. No one buys a **Mercedes** sports car just because it's fast and reliable – they buy it because it looks beautiful outside and looks, feels and smells terrific inside. For James Seddon, the look of the product is not as important as whether it works well. Yet he cannot ignore the aesthetics altogether. If it looks cheap, people will expect it to be cheap to buy (and may doubt whether it will work). James intends the first Eggxactly product to be black and chrome, to look classy and to look like a serious piece of kitchen equipment.

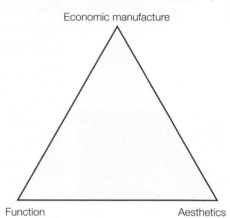

The design mix

Design and product differentiation

Product differentiation means making your product stand out from the competition. Making people see it as really different and distinctive. This may help the product become a market leader, as *The Sun* is within the British newspaper market. Or, like **BMW**, the distinctiveness may allow high prices to be charged, but without ever becoming a huge-selling product. Table 8.1 gives some more examples.

High differentiation is important because customers can become loyal to something that they see as different, even unique. Most *Sun* readers buy that paper and that paper alone; most iPod users would buy a new iPod if their original one was lost or stolen.

Design plays a crucial part in this process. It starts with a brand logo, such as the **Nike** 'Swoosh' (the tick). This makes products recognisable

Product differentiation

MARKET	DIFFERENTIATED PRODUCT
Cars	BMW
MP3 players	iPod
Newspapers	*The Sun*
Drinking yoghurt	Yakult

in a shop and when worn. In many cases there are other key characteristics. As a Merc sweeps past, it is usually recognisable without seeing the badge on the bonnet. Its designers try to keep all Mercs looking as if they are from the same family of cars.

A well-designed product will stand out from the crowd and will make the user take pride in using it/wearing it. That will help in achieving product differentiation.

Research and development

Every business needs to think about how to do things better and to make better things. This is where R&D becomes important. The R stands for Research. This does not mean market research. It is scientific research, such as James Seddon with his soft-polymer plastics. In effect, it is white-coat, laboratory science – experiments with new materials or chemicals. The D stands for Development. Engineers are needed to take a new idea and then see how it could be put into practice. This involves designing the machines to make the product and designing the factory to produce it.

Today there is increasingly tough competition from abroad, especially for producing low-cost goods. Clever firms try to keep one or two steps ahead by inventing new ways of working. Spending on R&D helps in this process.

Conclusion

It is hard to run a business if competition is too direct or too fierce. A business has fixed overhead costs such as rent and salaries, so enthusiastic price-cutting by a competitor is very threatening. If you cannot make money at the prices being charged in the marketplace, you may be driven out of business.

This is why every firm wants to be differentiated from its rivals. Design is an important way to achieve this. It can give customers what they want – stylish, modern but practical products – yet at the same time give the producer what it wants – a degree of security.

Revision essentials
Aesthetics: appeals to the senses, such as products that look, smell or feel good.
Patent: registering a new way of making something, so that no one can copy the idea for 20 years.

Exercises

Read the unit, then ask yourself:

1 Briefly explain how James Seddon made use of these two factors to help design the Eggxactly egg cooker: an understanding of science, an understanding of the market. (6)

2 What is the importance in product design of 'economic manufacture'? (2)

3 Discuss how McDonald's might use the design mix to help it develop a new 'Olympian Burger' for 2012. (6)

4 How can design be used to differentiate:

    a a pair of Diesel jeans from other brands on the market (3)

    b a bottle of Tesco shampoo from one from Sainsbury's. (3)

Practice questions

The portable high chair – Totseat

Edinburgh company Totseat has developed an innovative fabric highchair. Founding Director Rachel Jones came up with the original Totseat idea after her own experiences as a mother.

But to develop Totseat's design to perfection, she conducted extensive testing and research with several other families. 'The first Totseat prototype was made from the lining of my wedding dress and the second from a sheet,' says Jones. 'Nineteen versions later, and after more than 900 testing experiences, Totseat was born.'

The detailed research process, which majored on safety and adaptability, revealed that parents wanted to be able to take their babies to any cafe or restaurant, not just to 'child-friendly' places. Fabric highseats have been around since the 1950s but were far from perfect – the Totseat meets the needs of parents who want something easy to use and adaptable for every shape and size of chair. Parents also asked for a product that was compact, comfortable, durable, washable, stylish and, above all, safe for their children to sit in.

Taking the time and effort to understand the needs of customers to evolve the product's design has paid off, with leading UK and European retailers, including John Lewis and Mothercare, now selling Totseats. The product also recently won the Grand Prix at the Scottish Design Awards.

Source: Design Council website: www.design-council.org.uk

Questions

1 Explain why a mother might have confidence that Totseat will work effectively. (4)

2 Is it possible for a business to take too much time and care over design? Explain your answer. (4)

3 Outline two key elements in Rachel Jones's approach to designing Totseat's product range. (4)

4 Totseat products are now distributed in more than 100 shops in Britain. Discuss the importance of design in this success story. (8)

9   Managing stock

Why stock management is difficult

In early December 2006 the **Nintendo** Wii was launched in Britain. The **stock** of 50,000 units was sold out within 12 hours, leaving thousands of gamers disappointed. Without stock, sales cannot happen. So manufacturers and **retailers** have to make sure they supply the right amount of goods to keep the shelves full.

Yet simply ordering lots of stock carries other risks for shopkeepers. Products that are expected to sell well may flop in the marketplace. In January 2007 it was easy to buy the Creative Zen MP3 player. It was widely available at £59.99 because shops had too much stock. It had been expected to make a dent in sales of the iPod, but customers stayed loyal to the **Apple** product. So shops had too much stock and had to start slashing the price.

As consumers, we are hugely demanding and quite intolerant. We expect to find every product we are looking for in stock, whenever we want it. Yet the retailers have to find a balance between too little stock and too much. If all they do is keep masses of stock of every item, their costs will be too high to stay in business. As shown in the figure below, even Britain's top supermarket chains struggle to achieve 100 per cent stock availability.

> '*Why should a customer wait weeks if he can buy from someone else's shelf?*'
>
> Anon

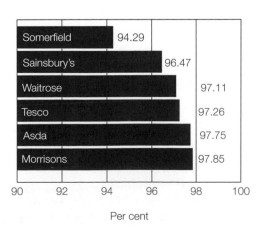

Stock problems at Britain's leading supermarkets: shelf availability of stock, Jan-Dec 2006 (Reproduced by permission of The Grocer, © William Reed Publishing Ltd 2006)

Stock graphs

Successful stock management requires the right balance between reliability and cost. Too little stock and customers can be let down. Too much stock and high costs will force high prices (or losses and potential closure).

The traditional approach is shown in the graph below. It illustrates how stock levels should ideally be maintained. It is based on three things:

1 The level of demand for the product. If it's a popular item, plenty will need to be kept in stock and orders for fresh supplies may have to be sent regularly.

2 **A decision on the right level of buffer stock**. This is the minimum amount of stock the manager thinks should be held at all times. For example, a busy sweetshop might like to keep a minimum of one box of Cadbury Dairy Milk in stock (48 bars) as customers expect to always find it on the counter.

3 **A decision on how often to order from the supplier, e.g. weekly or monthly**. A monthly order would be four times the size of a weekly order and might therefore provide bulk-buying benefits.

Take, for example, the management of stocks of Heinz Beans at Bob's Grocery. He has steady sales of 20 cans a week and likes to buy 4 boxes of beans at a time, each containing 20 cans. This is because when he buys 4 boxes his supplier gives him an extra 10 per cent discount. He chooses to keep a minimum of 10 cans in stock at all times (his buffer stock).

The graph below shows how the delivery of 80 cans pushes his stock up from 10 to 90. Then, as shoppers steadily buy the cans, stock slips down from 90 to 70, then down to 50, then 30, then 10. At this point he needs a new batch of 80 cans, which pushes the stock back up to 90. As long as customers keep buying 20 cans a week and the supplier delivers on time, this process will go on working smoothly.

Graphs such as this one are built into the scanning software used by many shops. When the barcode scanner shows that stocks of baked beans have fallen to ten tins, it can either flash a warning to the shopkeeper or reorder automatically from the supplier.

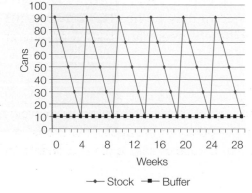

Stock (bar gate) graph for Heinz beans at Bob's Grocery

Just In Time

Buffer stocks help ensure that customers always find what they want on the shelf. Yet they not only cost money, they also use up space. Ten years ago, a supermarket might have used up 20 per cent of its floor space in stockrooms. These rooms were closed off from the public, just holding stocks. **Tesco** was one of the first stores to recognise that this was a terrible waste. Why not turn the stock room into an extra sales floor, perhaps to stock non-food items such as clothes?

So Tesco started insisting that suppliers should deliver more frequently, but in smaller quantities. Therefore there was less need for a big storage room. Furthermore it started using 'Just In Time' (JIT). This means ordering extra supplies 'just in time' before the old supplies run out. In other words it does away with a buffer stock. Tesco believes it is so efficient that it does not need a buffer. It will order the right quantities at the right time. The table on page 37 shows that even Britain's most successful retailer runs out of stock from time to time (2.74 per cent of the time, to be precise). Yet clearly its managers find that the benefits of Just In Time outweigh the costs of lower customer satisfaction.

Advantages and disadvantages of Just In Time

ADVANTAGES OF JIT	DISADVANTAGES OF JIT
Eliminating buffer stocks cuts storage space, allowing more sales space.	A greater risk of running out of stock and therefore disappointing customers.
Low stocks and frequent supplier deliveries mean fresher produce.	Buying smaller quantities more often means losing out on bulk-buying discounts.
Less of the business's capital is tied up in stocks.	Any mistake or misjudgement could cause out-of-stocks and poorer customer service.

Conclusion

Managing stocks is difficult to get right. All it takes is for Jamie Oliver to mention 'pukka Thai noodles' one night on TV and the shelves of Britain will be empty by 10am the next day. If a business sets its sights on providing fantastic customer service, it may need to set high buffer stocks to ensure that no shelf is ever empty. If, however, the business (like Primark, Aldi or Lidl) is focused on low prices, low stocks and a JIT system may be needed to keep costs down. Different firms have different needs and therefore different policies.

Revision essentials

Buffer (stock): the minimum stock level held at all times to avoid running out.

Retailers: businesses that sell goods to the public, i.e. shops.

Stock(s): items held by a firm for use or sale, e.g. components for manufacturing, or sellable products for a retailer.

Exercises

Read the unit, then ask yourself:

1 Look at the bar chart on page 37 and answer these questions:
   a Which supermarket ran out of stock 2.15 per cent of the time? (1)
   b Which supermarket ran out of stock 5.71 per cent of the time? (1)
   c What impact might this have on customers' loyalty to each of these stores? (4)

2 Outline one reason why a small grocer's shop might set:
   a a low buffer stock for fresh grapes (2)
   b a high buffer stock for Cadbury's Creme Eggs. (2)

3 Look at the graph on page 38 and answer these questions:
   a In what way does the graph show that Bob wants to keep ten cans in stock at all times? (1)
   b What is the maximum number of cans of beans held in stock? (1)
   c Explain what the graph would show if Bob's supplier forgot to deliver the 80 tins of beans. (5)

4 Give two reasons why a factory owner might be worried about ordering raw materials on a JIT basis. (2)

5 Take one of the disadvantages of JIT shown in the table on page 39. Explain how it might affect sales at
   a a shoe shop in a busy shopping centre (3)
   b The Manchester United Club Shop, Old Trafford. (3)

Practice questions

Caught short

Supermarkets have been running out of basic items in the run-up to Christmas. Shoppers have found staples such as bread and milk missing from shelves, according to a survey released yesterday. It found that stock levels at the big six – Tesco, Sainsbury's, Asda, Morrisons, Somerfield and Waitrose – have deteriorated over the past six months. The survey, by *The Grocer* magazine, was based on weekly checks on the availability and price of 33 commonly purchased items.

The magazine's Gaele Walker said: 'Availability levels in the UK's top six supermarkets have plummeted over the past six months. Somerfield's performance was by far the weakest, with 48 "out-of-stocks" – 22 more than previously.' Items missing from Somerfield's shelves over the past 26 weeks included apple juice, oranges, Wall's sausages, Cathedral City cheddar and Andrex toilet tissue.

Sainsbury's was out of 30 staples over the same period including frozen peas, four-pint containers of semi-skimmed milk and baguettes. The top three chains, in order, were Morrison's, which was out of 18 products, Asda and Tesco.

The survey yielded some good news for Asda which was found to be the cheapest of the chains for the cost of buying the 33 basic items. Tesco ranked second, with Morrisons and Sainsbury's vying for third place. Most expensive were Somerfield and Waitrose.

Source: Sean Poulter, Daily Mail, 18 December 2006

Questions

1 Explain the meaning of the term 'stock levels'. (3)

2 Somerfield ran out of oranges while Sainsbury's ran short of frozen peas.

  a Why might the buffer stock level for frozen peas be set at a higher level than for oranges? (3)

  b Why, then, should Sainsbury's be criticised more for running out of peas than Somerfield for running out of oranges? (4)

3 Somerfield has the lowest market share of the major supermarkets. Its prices are the highest and stock levels are the lowest. Discuss which of these two urgent problems it should tackle first. (10)

10 Managing quality

Introduction

Quality is the ultimate test of a business organisation. Do customers who arrive or phone or email have a positive experience? For producers of goods, quality is about practical matters such as reliability. For service businesses, quality is often about personal things such as polite staff.

Hitachi recently increased the **warranty** period on its personal computers from one to three years. A new quality management system gave it the confidence to do this. Customers, of course, were delighted – boosting sales and market share.

With restaurants, quality is partly to do with the product (is it well cooked and served hot?) but also to do with the service: are staff friendly, well trained and on the customer's side? A customer who leaves feeling angry will never return; even a weakly positive response may not be enough. To return, we have to be thrilled. Customers should be delighted, not just satisfied.

> 'Quality is very simple. So simple, in fact, that it is difficult for people to understand.'
>
> Roger Hale, chief executive

Quality control

Many firms regard quality as a management issue, to be controlled by careful systems. Managers may put in place practices such as:

- factory inspectors at the end of a production line, who check every fifth car or carpet before it's sent to the customer; if several cars fail to start, they might decide to check the whole day's output; any faults found are corrected
- a 100 per cent inspection system, just as Gordon Ramsay does in his restaurants: the head chef checks every plate before it's sent to the high-paying customers; if the steak is slightly burnt, Ramsay throws away the whole plate of food and demands that his chefs start again
- a feedback system, such as a customer feedback questionnaire, which you might find in a hotel room or be given at an airport. This is a check on the final experience enjoyed or suffered by the customer.

The problem all these systems share is that they rarely feel part of the life of the worker. A car worker who is putting left front doors on Minis all day long cannot even see the end of the line where the inspectors are checking the quality. Similarly, the hotel cleaning staff do not see the feedback questionnaire responses – indeed they may rarely see a hotel guest. Only in the Ramsay kitchen does the chef see his cooking thrown away in disgust by an angry head chef.

Most systems of **quality control**, therefore, are flawed. They try to put a lid on a problem rather than solve it. They work on the basis of 'acceptable' quality. In effect, they accept that staff will not think much about quality, therefore the managers have to 'sort it out'.

> 'It is quality rather than quantity that matters.'
> Publilius Syrus, Roman writer 42 BC

Quality culture

In the ideal business, quality is fundamental to everyone's attitude to work. If you're going to an ice cream parlour, what you want is someone behind the counter who delights in offering you free samples of 'two terrific new flavours' – and enjoys building up the ice cream on the cone to make it look great. When you go to **Next**, you want the staff to really help you find something that fits well, rather than look frustrated when you don't buy the first couple of things you try on. Ideally, everyone would be enjoying their job of serving you.

Business **culture** means the general attitudes and behaviours among staff within a workplace. Years ago, the **Arsenal** dressing room was famous for a hard-drinking, hard-gambling culture. Then came new boss Arsene Wenger, who steadily transformed the culture to a passion for sporting excellence, rather than excess. Successful businesses ensure that a quality culture develops among staff. This would come from pride in the business and what it does for its customers.

In Japan, **Toyota** recruits only graduates for its factory floor jobs. It wants engineers who gain experience of what car production is all about before they get promoted to supervisory or management jobs. Toyota wants its workers to spend their days thinking about how the process can be made more efficient and how quality can be improved. In this way, Toyota has risen to overtake Ford as the world's second biggest car producer – and from 2007 it will be the world's Number One. The culture of quality that is famous at Toyota (and Honda) has helped these Japanese companies dominate quality surveys in America and Britain for years.

JD Power 2006 UK car customer satisfaction index

Top 5	Bottom 5
1 Lexus (Toyota)	1 (Worst) Citroen
2 Honda	2 Land Rover (Ford)
3 Skoda (Volkswagen)	3 Mitsubishi
4 Toyota	4 Peugeot
5 BMW	5 MG Rover

How to develop a culture of quality

When Tim Waterstone started the **Waterstone's** bookshops, he allowed every store manager the freedom to create his or her own store. One in London had a huge children's book section because the manager was a young mother. She and her staff took pride in the fact that families would travel from all over London to visit that shop. And all the staff loved talking to young children about what they liked to read. Other Waterstone's branches focused on books on sport, or cookery, or science fiction.

This approach was brilliant because quality develops when staff get satisfaction from their jobs. If they believe in what they are doing, believe in the products they are selling and care about their customers, quality has arrived.

To develop a quality culture, new staff must learn from the start about the high standards expected from everyone. Those standards must be set every day by every manager, so that no one doubts that they are real. If a customer returns an ice cream that was melted and then refrozen, a good manager will check the rest of the batch and if she or he finds them all ruined, will take them all off sale. This sets the standard for all staff.

In a school, a quality culture will be seen in a staffroom where teachers talk about the successes of the students – on the hockey pitch or in the classroom. In other schools staff moan about the students or talk about anything other than work.

> 'They didn't want it good. They wanted it Thursday.'
> Ronald Reagan, movie actor turned President of the USA, talking about early movie producers he had worked for

Conclusion

High quality is achieved by providing an efficient service: the right product of the right quality at the right time – with a human face. This is hard to attain 100 per cent of the time because mistakes happen. The best way to achieve it is to establish a culture of quality based on motivated staff who care about the customers and about the company's reputation.

Once the culture is established, further quality controls may not be necessary. For example, if a fully qualified surgeon is carrying out an operation, no one else will peer over his or her shoulder to check on the quality. He or she is trusted. However, at Gordon Ramsay restaurants and at Toyota car factories, further inspections are carried out to make 100 per cent sure that the quality is spot on. So a combination of quality culture and quality control is probably the best of all worlds.

Exercises
(20 marks; 20 minutes)

Read the unit, then ask yourself:

1 Explain how 'customer delight' might affect a firm's sales. (3)
2 Outline one possible weakness in a quality control system based on factory inspectors checking a sample of the finished product before it's sent to customers. (2)
3 MG Rover went out of business in early 2005. How may the customer satisfaction figures revealed in the above table have affected the business? (4)
4 At school, you and your parents are 'customers'. Outline one example of good and one example of poor quality service that you or your parents experience from the school. (6)
5 Explain why highly motivated staff are more likely to deliver high-quality service. (5)

Practice Exercises
(20 marks; 25 minutes)

The cornerstone of Toyota's quality control system is the role of the team members in the production process. The principles on which Toyota was founded are employed at the Georgetown plant, USA. Toyota involves its team members by:

- encouraging an active role in quality control
- utilising employee ideas and opinions in production processes
- striving for constant improvement (called *kaizen* in Japan).

New-product planning emphasises a product that is as defect-free as possible. In other words, Toyota designs quality into the automobile. Then Toyota's quality control during production ensures that the correct materials and parts are used and fitted with precision and accuracy. This effort is combined with thousands of rigorous inspections performed by team members during the production process.

Team members on the line are responsible for the parts they use. They are inspectors for their own work and that of co-workers. When a problem on any vehicle is spotted, any team member can pull a rope – called an andon cord – strung along the assembly line to halt production. Only when the problem is resolved is the line restarted. This process involves every team member in monitoring and checking the quality of every car produced.

Questions

1 a Identify three ways in which Toyota is ensuring high-quality output.   (3)

  b Briefly outline the benefits of these methods to Toyota customers.   (3)

2 From this text plus the table, explain how Toyota may be benefiting from the high-quality standards it achieves.   (6)

3 Discuss whether Toyota's quality management at Georgetown is based upon quality control or a quality culture.   (8)

11 Cost-effective operations

In early 2007 **Ford of America** announced that it planned to cut its US costs by £1000 per car. This would involve cutting 14,000 office jobs and closing 16 factories. The total cost saving aimed to be more than £2500 million per year. This became necessary because Ford's sales had been slipping for some years, pushing the company into huge losses. The rise of Toyota and the fall in sales of Ford's gas-guzzling trucks were largely to blame.

Even companies as massive as Ford have to make sure that they keep costs low enough to be competitive. If **Toyota** is offering a luxurious, fuel-efficient family car for $18,000 (about £9500), Ford has to make sure that its production costs are low enough to do the same. If it costs Ford $20,000 to make each car, everything it sells will be at a loss.

The same is true for a local builder. If he has to charge £1000 for building a wall but a rival can do it for £700, there is only one possible result: the more expensive builder must either give up or find a way to operate at a lower cost.

Keeping costs down

What are the costs involved in building a brick wall?

1   **Materials**: bricks and cement. These must be ordered in the right quantity and at the lowest prices available from suppliers.
2   **Other costs directly involved**: hiring a cement mixer for a day or two; hiring a skip for the building waste.
3   **Labour**: this is a function of the amount of work involved, the hourly wage of the workers and the productivity of those workers.
4   **Fixed costs**: the fixed costs of the management time taken to win the order, supervise the work and deal with office administration.

'The three most important things right now are costs, costs and costs. And costs can be summed up in one word: productivity.'
Financial Analyst, *New York Times*

To keep costs to the minimum, careful ordering of materials and other supplies is very important. Every business, though, will be trying to buy at the lowest price and making sure not to buy more than is needed to complete a job. Therefore cost savings through purchasing are rarely crucial.

> 'People are most productive in small teams ... and the freedom to solve their own problems.'
> John Rollwagen, CEO, Cray Research

Far more important is good management of labour costs. Labour costs per hour vary dramatically in different parts of the world (see the table below). The figures show that, in 2006, a firm could employ 32 workers in India for every one in Britain. Even within the European Union the differences can be stark, with new entrant Romania having average earnings that are less than one tenth of the British level.

Weekly average earnings*
(based on 40-hour weeks)

Germany	£505
Britain	£485
South Korea	£325
Czech Republic	£100
Romania	£45
China (in towns)	£23
India	£15

*Median average earnings; source: Federation of European Employers, April 2006

For companies to keep employing workers in Britain, they must find a way to get value out of the high wages being paid. This could come about if British workers have skills that cannot be found elsewhere – for example, the ability to write computer games or deal in foreign exchange. Or people can be worth the money they are paid if they are highly productive; in other words they produce a lot of work in the time they are employed. This means having high productivity.

Gavin is a bricklayer. He can lay 800 bricks in a day and is paid £120 per day. His friend John is a builder who is skilled at many different tasks (plastering, flooring, carpentry), but he can only lay 400 bricks a day. So, if both are paid £120 for a day's work:

	Pay	Output	Labour cost per brick
Gavin	£120	800	15p (£120/800 = £0.15)
John	£120	400	30p

Productivity is efficiency, usually measured as output per person. In this case, Gavin is twice as productive as John, therefore John is twice as expensive to hire, from the point of view of a company. High productivity enables the labour cost to be spread across lots of output. Low productivity (John) means higher labour costs per unit.

Productivity differences can be much bigger than this. In 1999, **Renault** bought the Romanian car business **Dacia**. It employed 27,000 people and made 110,000 cars a year. In the same year the **Nissan** factory in Sunderland, UK, was producing 270,000 cars with just 2750 people. Therefore the productivity difference was:

	Staff	Output (cars)	Productivity (cars per worker per year)
Dacia	27,000	110,000	4 cars per year
Nissan	2750	270,000	98 cars per year

Even at the much lower wage rates in Romania, it was far better value to manufacture cars in Britain, although since 1999, of course, Renault has set out to change this.

In general, higher productivity is one of the keys to success when up against competition. Ways of increasing productivity include:

- investing in up-to-date machinery to help workers work faster, or to replace them with **automated** equipment or robots
- encouraging workers to work more enthusiastically and therefore harder and faster; this can be achieved through improved morale and motivation
- encouraging staff to work smarter – to come up with new ways to do things more effectively. Toyota says it receives more than 100,000 employee suggestions per year.

> 'The best way to have a good idea is to have a lot of ideas.'
> Linus Pauling, Nobel prize winner

Keeping the business competitive

If high **productivity** keeps costs per unit down, a firm can compete. As shown in the following figure, if **Ryanair** cuts its prices, **easyJet** can compete, but **British Airways** will struggle. Ryanair and British Airways carry the same number of passengers – but BA has staff costs that are nearly 20 times higher!

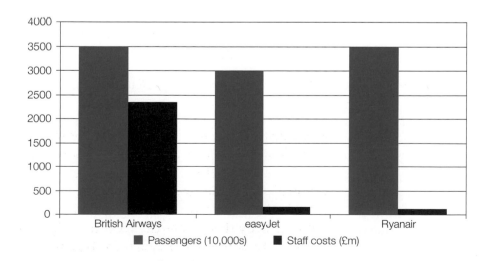

Passenger numbers compared with staffing costs. Source: Annual Report and Accounts 2005/2006 for these three companies

Conclusion

A well-managed business keeps a careful eye on efficiency. This is especially important for firms competing with overseas suppliers. While France and Germany may have higher wage costs than Britain, many other countries have remarkably low-cost workforces. In the long run, every country, every company and every employee in Britain will need to be a bit special to keep successful.

Revision essentials

Automated: processes that are fully carried out by machinery rather than people.

Productivity: efficiency, measured by output per worker

Exercises

(20 marks; 20 minutes)

Read the unit, then ask yourself:

1 Toyota can sell a car for $18,000 that costs Ford $20,000 to make. In this situation, how might productivity improvements help Ford? (3)

2 **a** Bartex Ltd, a small lighting factory, employs 150 staff and has a monthly output of 180,000 lamps. What is the factory's monthly productivity? (3)

   b A rival based in Hull pays similar wages and has monthly productivity of 1500 lamps. Outline two ways this might affect Bartex. (4)

3 Gavin is twice as productive as John. Give three possible reasons why this may be the case. (3)

4 Explain how improved staff motivation might affect productivity. (3)

5 Outline two ways in which Renault may have tried to improve productivity at Dacia since 1999. (4)

Practice questions

(20 marks; 25 minutes)

The plastic microchip

In January 2007 Plastic Logic, a Cambridge-based company, announced that it was setting up a £50 million factory in Dresden, eastern Germany. The factory would be the world's first producer of microchips made from plastic instead of silicon. This could cut the price of microchips by 90 per cent, making every electronic product much cheaper – from iPods to PS3s to computers. The factory would employ 140 people when it opened in late 2008.

But why would a Cambridge company (with an invention that came from Cambridge University) set up its factory in eastern Germany? The reason was because the workforce was highly skilled and very committed. Plastic Logic carried out some trial interviews in Dresden, Singapore and New York. The German workers were the most enthusiastic and the best qualified. Wage rates are higher in Dresden than in Singapore or Britain, but the company felt productivity would be highest in Germany.

Questions

1 What is meant by the term 'productivity'? (2)

2 Explain how productivity will be affected by staff being: enthusiastic, highly skilled. (6)

3 Explain why high productivity can make high wages more affordable for an employer. (6)

4 Discuss whether the owners of Plastic Logic should be paid by the British government to keep the factory and jobs in Britain. (6)

Effective customer service

It had already been an unlucky day for four teenage **Wigan** supporters on 13 January 2007. Chelsea had just beaten their team 4–0, with the Wigan defence handing out presents like a bunch of Santas. Then they missed the Supporters' Club coach home from Stamford Bridge and were left with hardly a penny between them. They sat down and wept. Fortunately the Wigan players saw them, had a whip round which collected over £200, and sent them home to Lancashire. That's **customer service**.

This marked a big turn-round for the club. Just two months before, manager Paul Jewell had criticised the fans for staying away. Home attendances had slumped. Then the club started to talk to its supporters (the customers). For the pre-Christmas home game against Chelsea the ticket price was halved to £15 – and the ground was packed. With loud support behind them, Wigan were unlucky to lose 3–2. The Boxing Day derby against Blackburn saw ticket prices move back up and attendance slump by 7000.

By early January, though, the club realised that some ticket prices had to be cut down to £15 (Portsmouth, West Ham and Middlesbrough) and others to £20 (Newcastle and Spurs). The club was finally providing an effective customer service.

To be effective, customer service must be:

- rooted in a clear understanding of what customers really care about
- practical and cost-effective enough to ensure that it can be kept going regularly
- based on a genuine wish to help, rather than the attempt to seem helpful
- offered at the right time in the right way at the right place.

> 'People perform best, and give the best customer service, when they like what they do.'
>
> Anon

Making it efficient

Good customer service is designed for the customer, not the company. It is efficient because it works well, works quickly and gives the customer the sense of being cared for. A call to the school is answered by the school secretary who knows that the head is out today. With bad service, a call puts you into a voicemail loop and you wait several minutes listening to tinny 1970s' music. Only then do you get through to someone at a call centre 25 – or 10,000 – miles away. That person knows nothing about the school, or the head teacher.

Efficient service:

- gets products to you exactly when you want them
- in good condition …
- … but if there is something wrong, it will be sorted as soon as possible and in the right spirit (if you leave a jacket in a shop, it would be great for them to contact you, instead of you having to figure out which shop you left it in).

Good service may cost the customer extra, but that is fine as long as it represents value for money.

Good customer service must relate to what customers want and what they are willing to pay for. A discounted 'Upper Class' flight on **Virgin Atlantic** to New York costs £2800 return. This is about ten times the cost of a standard class ticket. For that you get a seat that doubles as a bed, an on-board massage and better food. It is hard to see that this *can* be value for money – yet some people (or their companies) are happy to pay it.

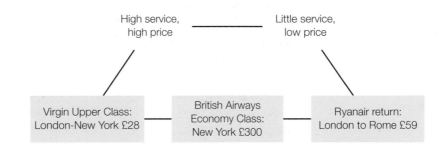

Ryanair, meanwhile, offers no 'customer service'. Boss Michael O'Leary boasts his contempt for the way most airlines offer service frills rather than the real thing. If you put 'Ryanair customer service' into Google you get over 400,000 items. Most are hostile about the 'scrum to get a seat', 'not even a cup of tea', or 'charging you to put a bag on the plane!' O'Leary, though, would point to some important facts. Ryanair is Europe's most punctual airline. If all you want is to get cheaply, quickly and efficiently to Spain and back, Ryanair is for you, as you can see in the table below.

Airline punctuality January–September 2006

	% of planes arriving more than one hour late
Ryanair	4.2%
British Airways	6.4%
easyJet	7.1%
Virgin Atlantic	9.4%

Bad customer service

In the past, bad customer service was sloppy because it risked losing a customer. These days, **YouTube** and many other websites have made bad service potentially suicidal. If the family is going out for a birthday restaurant meal, mum or dad will probably check out www.toptable.co.uk. A glance at the 'latest reviews' posted by customers shows up a 23 January 2007 review of a London restaurant called *Palm Court Brasserie:* 'Food was lovely but service was slow and sporadic and the waiter forgot two things. Nice atmosphere but toilets were rank.'

Word of mouth is always an important factor, as people love to talk about their holiday or eating-out disasters and successes. Today, though, the internet has made it so much quicker and easier for bad news to spread.

Staff need to be trained not only to provide good service but also how to cope when things go wrong – what to do when the steak ordered well-done has been left, bloody, on the plate (quietly apologise, say it won't be charged for and offer a free alternative). Intelligent, generous service can turn a disaster into a bit of a triumph, with the customer going away really impressed.

> 'There is only one boss: the customer. And he can fire everyone in the company, from the chairman on down, simply by spending his money somewhere else.'
>
> Sam Walton, founder of the multi-billion retailer, Wal-Mart

Customer service and repeat purchase

For the business, the reason to provide great customer service is because it keeps customers coming back. In business, nothing beats **repeat purchase**. It can cost a lot of money to persuade someone to try something new. Advertisers believe that people need to see a TV commercial at least five times before it has an effect on attitudes. Five national TV commercials on ITV can easily cost £400,000. So it is madness to risk losing these people through poor service.

Some families return year after year to the same hotel in Brighton or Biarritz. They like to feel confident that they will always be welcomed and always served well. Some go to the same pub because the staff are always friendly. Repeat custom adds to revenue, cuts marketing costs and therefore can multiply profits.

Revision essentials

Customer service: the way in which a business acts (or fails to act) to provide what the customer is looking for.

Repeat purchase: when customers not only try a product or service but come back for more.

Exercises

(20 marks; 25 minutes)

Read the unit, then ask yourself:

1 Explain the importance of:

    a rooting customer service 'in a clear understanding of what customers really care about'. (4)

    b designing customer service 'for the customer, not the company'. (4)

2 Explain how Ryanair might be said to provide good customer service. (4)

3 You and your family are spending a night at a hotel in Scotland, as there is a family wedding the following day. You get there, tired and hungry, to be told by the receptionist: 'No, we have no record of a booking in your name. And all we have is one single room. You'll have to squeeze in there ... and the restaurant closes in ten minutes, so you'd better be quick.'

    a Outline two faults in the quality of the receptionist's service. (4)

    b Outline two possible impacts on the hotel that may be a consequence of this incident. (4)

Practice questions

(20 marks; 25 minutes)

In June 2006 *HolidayTravelWatch* had to deal with a mass of complaints about the Miramar holiday resort in Obzor, Bulgaria. It is used extensively by Britain's biggest tour operator, Thomson Holidays.

The problems began at the end of June, when serious flooding caused the sewage system to fail. Holidaymakers were evacuated to clear up the mess, but the same people were returned to the hotel a few days later. One report from a holidaymaker said that 'the swimming pool was full of sludge and it was difficult to find the exact position of the pool because of the extent of the flooding'. A newly arrived visitor 'could not understand why everything seemed damp and he has reported finding an infestation of flies, mosquitoes and frogs on the balcony of his room'.

Over the following months, there were repeated complaints about stomach bugs requiring medical treatment. Despite many protests, travellers were advised by the tour operator that their health problems stemmed from an 'airborne virus' and that the hotel had passed its health and safety check.

The Managing Director of the *HolidayTravelWatch* website later said: 'This major tour operator appears to have ignored the common sense approach to this problem. Instead of abandoning the hotel and taking care of their customers, they have compounded the problem by adding fresh holiday victims to this appalling situation.'

In January 2007, the hotel was still being promoted by Thomson Holidays, describing it as 'opulent'.

Source: adapted from www.holidaytravel watch.com

Questions

1 Examine one reason why this tour operator might have acted in the way it did. (4)

2 Discuss how the tour operator should have handled the situation following the flooding. (8)

3 Examine the possible longer-term effects of these events upon the tour operator. (8)

13 Consumer protection

Starting a business is easy. You just let the Inland Revenue know, then get on with it. Turning it into a meaningful, long-term investment, though, is harder. You have to build a base of loyal customers who want to spend their money with you.

When **Manchester City** were relegated twice, ending up playing Carlisle instead of Chelsea, 30,000 supporters turned up every week. And kept buying the shirts, the scarves and the pies. A hairdresser needs the same, so even if you're a bit disappointed with one haircut, you return a month later. Fundamentally, you see it as *your* hairdresser.

If all businesses worked this way, we would not need laws to protect the consumer. Unfortunately, it is not quite like that. Although many small firms do their best to build customer loyalty, others are not so careful.

This might be for the following reasons:

- The business is in a **monopoly** position, i.e. it has no competition and therefore becomes sloppy. Hygiene standards at a college canteen might slacken, with customers moaning but still buying – until an outbreak of food poisoning.
- A large business in a competitive market allows its ethical standards to slip, i.e. managers make decisions that could not be defended morally.
- Individual business owners get greedy and are unable to resist an opportunity to make big profits in the short term.

On 18 December 2006, *Julie's* restaurant in posh Holland Park, London, was fined £7500 for swindling famous customers such as Kate Moss, Kylie Minogue and U2. The menu had boasted of 'organic, marinated roast chicken', 'organic sausages' and 'organic lamb'. But it was a lie. Environmental health officers found that none of the meat sold in the restaurant over a two-month period was organic. During October and November 2005 the restaurant had saved itself £4186 just on the chicken. As *The Independent* newspaper put it: they 'bought cheap meat and pocketed the change'. A local councillor said: 'Customers have a right to receive what is advertised on the menu. For many visitors to the restaurant, this has led to a betrayal of lifestyle.'

> 'If there were no bad people there would be no good lawyers.'
> Charles Dickens

Key consumer protection laws

Sale of Goods Act

Originally passed in 1893, this Act is one of the world's earliest examples of a law passed by Parliament to protect the consumer. It has been updated many times, the latest being 1994. This is the Act that gives you the right to take back a faulty item and get your money back, e.g. the dress in which the zip gets stuck the second time it's worn, or the vacuum cleaner that breaks down after six months.

The key features of the Sale of Goods Act are:

- goods must be fit for the purpose for which they are sold
- relevant aspects of 'fit for purpose' include freedom from defects, the appearance, finish, **durability** and safety
- the buyer has a right to get his/her money back, or could choose to have it repaired at the seller's expense
- the person responsible for correcting any problem is the seller (the shop), not the manufacturer.

The Act is not stupid, as it accepts that low-cost items may wear out quickly. If you buy a £1.99 umbrella, do not expect the Act to get your money back four months later. In other instances, however, the Act will accept compensation claims up to six years from the purchase date. So faults in a brand new house might give rise to a claim for refund five years after the purchase date.

Trades Descriptions Act

The owners of *Julie's* restaurant were breaking the Trades Descriptions Act when they called chicken 'organic' when it was not. This Act (passed in 1968) put an end to 100 years of misleading advertisements. Before the Act, Guinness said 'Guinness is Good For You', dogfood PAL claimed to 'Prolong Active Life' and – much earlier – brands of cigarettes claimed to be healthy, such as 'Heartsease' – good for your heart.

The Trades Descriptions Act insists that all advertising, pack labels and public statements made by firms about their products must be 'demonstrably true'. In other words, there must be evidence for them.

Key features include:

- it is an offence for a trader to use false or misleading statements
- it is an offence to misleadingly label goods and services
- the Act carries criminal penalties and can therefore lead to a jail sentence.

Although specific statements must be provable, e.g. that Yakult helps the digestion, advertisers can still get away with clever ways round the Act. Many of the claims about Omega-3 have little scientific support. Manufacturers of foods containing Omega-3 keep mentioning 'the brain' in their advertising, even though they cannot claim that Omega-3 makes children cleverer.

Despite the tricks some companies use, there is no doubt that the Trades Descriptions Act has reduced substantially the number of customers being conned by suppliers.

Other key Acts

Among many other Acts passed to protect consumers are:

- the Consumer Credit Act (1974): every item sold on credit must have a clear indication of the APR – the annualised percentage interest rate – being charged
- the Weights and Measures Act 1985 (updated in 2006): if the bag says 500 grammes, that is what it must contain
- the Food Safety Act (1990): to prevent illness from eating food sold to the public, by insisting that sales staff have hygiene training and that premises are inspected regularly.

It is not important to remember these other Acts. However, it is important to know that there are more than just the two main Acts. This is because firms often complain that they are overwhelmed by the amount of legislation they must learn to cope with.

Are firms held back by legislation?

In 2006 the Federation of Small Businesses carried out research among the owners of small firms. The results showed that 50 per cent thought that excessive regulation would hinder their growth in the next few years. But are firms right to feel this way? After all, just as football managers have always got 'reasons' (excuses?) for their latest defeat, so it is possible that business owners like to blame government for their own failings.

Many businesses say:

- too many rules mean too much paperwork which costs time and money
- rules can restrict our creativity and initiative
- we don't mind rules that apply directly to us, but we object to '**red tape**' that we have to complete but isn't designed for 'firms like mine'.

Others argue that:

- it helps firms to know what is acceptable and what is not – that lets them concentrate on doing things better
- rules do take time and money, but not enough to damage firms' drive for success
- consumer protection law is too valuable to dismiss just because firms find it time-consuming; people can die from faulty drugs, unsafe cars or a dodgy kebab.

Revision essentials

Durability: how strong the product is and therefore how well and long it lasts.

Monopoly: when there is only one supplier, i.e. no competition, so one company has the market to itself, e.g. BAA with London airports (it owns Gatwick and Heathrow).

Red tape: implies tangling firms up in too many rules and regulations; stifling them.

Exercises

(15 marks; 15 minutes)

Read the unit, then ask yourself:

1 Explain why there would be no need for consumer laws if every business was aiming to build long-term customer loyalty. (4)

2 *Julie's* restaurant has had terrible publicity following its prosecution.

   a Outline two possible reasons why it pretended its meat was organic. (4)

   b Explain one reason why *Julie's* may be able to keep going, despite this setback. (3)

3 State whether the following incidents are covered by the Sale of Goods Act, the Trades Descriptions Act or neither:

   a A shop puts up a 'Sale' sign but doubles the prices before 'slashing them by 50%!'. (1)

   b A pair of running shoes splits open when the wearer is running fast, eight weeks after buying them. (1)

   c An advertisement promises that 'L'Oreal For Men will cure baldness in a week'. (1)

   d A 'Kate Moss' dress, bought last month, is condemned by *The Sun* as being 'more like last year's cast-offs than this year's fashion'. (1)

Practice questions

Prosecutions to protect consumers in South Ayrshire, Scotland

- On the 20th April 2005 a Greenock man was found guilty of offences under the Trade Descriptions Act 1968 and the Trade Marks Act 1994. The man had been selling counterfeit clothing and football tops at Ayr Sunday market.

- On the 24th May 2005 a Chinese lady was found guilty of selling counterfeit DVDs contrary to the Trade Descriptions Act 1968, the Trade Marks Act 1994 and the Video Recordings Act 1984. The woman was admonished by the court.

- On the 19th May 2004 a local jeweller was fined £400 after being found guilty of offences under the Trade Descriptions Act 1968. The jeweller had misled a local consumer into believing that a bangle she had supplied to her had been made by her from the consumer's own gold (as requested by the consumer). The bangle was in fact made of hollow gold and had been bought from a jewellery catalogue.

- On 15th March 2004 a farmer pled guilty to offences under the Cattle Database Regulations 1998, Trade Descriptions Act 1968 and the Cattle Identification Regulations 1998. The farmer had applied a false date of birth to a bullock, therefore making it over 30 months of age when presented for slaughter. He was fined £350 at Ayr Sheriff Court.

Source: South Ayrshire Council, www.south-ayrshire. gov.uk

Questions

1 Outline two possible reasons why the jeweller may have chosen to mislead the customer. (4)

2 All four prosecutions were for breaking the Trades Descriptions Act. Which of the four do you think was the worst and therefore deserved the harshest treatment? Explain your answer. (7)

3 To what extent do these examples prove the need for legislation to protect consumers? (9)

SECTION 3

EFFECTIVE FINANCIAL MANAGEMENT

14 How to improve cash flow

Helen and David Madueno-Jones opened their hotel in Andalucia in October 2006. At the time it felt like they had finally reached the end of a very long journey – they bought a plot of land in 2004 and then spent months negotiating planning permission, architects' plans and builders before finally arriving at opening day.

However, the real endurance test was just about to begin. Within a month of opening they were in trouble – they had more money going out of the business bank account than was coming in. Without swift action they risked losing everything they had worked for and more – David's parents had allowed the couple to use their own house as security for their loans.

Outflows and inflows

The couple first drew up a list of their outgoings (outflows). These included:

- mortgage repayments
- electricity
- car running costs
- wages for two staff
- laundry costs (bed linen from the hotel and table cloths and napkins from the restaurant)

- food supplies
- wine for restaurant
- beer and spirits
- advertising (specialist magazines).

Their income (cash inflows) was made up of hotel guests and customers in the restaurant. Their problem was how to improve their cash flow.

They first looked at how they could reduce their outgoings. When a business is struggling, laying off staff is the usual option. Helen and David were both working full time in the hotel and restaurant and employed two other full-time members of staff. A condition of their **EU grant** was that they employed four EU citizens – as they themselves were EU citizens they had to employ two other people, so laying people off was not an option. Also, with Christmas approaching they really needed more staff.

They considered cancelling their contract with the laundry but soon realised they could not manage the task themselves – they were rushed off their feet and had an eight-month-old baby.

They tried to find cheaper suppliers for their restaurant to cut costs that way but their unique selling point was that they used only fresh organic ingredients, so switching suppliers would mean their **USP** would be lost.

'In God we trust; all others pay cash.'

Anon

Overdraft

Helen and David took swift action with the bank at the end of their first trading month and negotiated a larger overdraft – in the short term this meant they could pay all their bills. Luckily the bank manager was a fan of the restaurant and agreed.

Credit terms

With Christmas and New Year fast approaching, the cash flow crisis could not have come at a worse time. Both the hotel and the restaurant were very busy and would not be able to function unless suppliers were paid. Helen and David chanced upon the solution when placing their order for wine and spirits for the festive period. The wine dealer offered them two months' credit (this meant they could have the supplies and pay for them two months later, allowing them to sell the items before paying for them). At last the couple had a chance to manage their cash flow better.

Christmas 2006 was their first festive season operating the hotel and restaurant, but despite the lifeline being given to them by one of their suppliers they still could not afford the extra staff they needed for the busy Christmas and New year period. Their solution was to call on family and friends who travelled down from Madrid and came from North Wales to help the couple out.

Payment from guests

Initially hotel guests were asked to pay a 50 per cent deposit on booking their room and paid the balance when checking out. Helen and David started asking for payment at the time of booking as another short-term solution to their cash flow problems.

Other ways to improve cash flow

Favourable customer credit

Antonia Krieger is a sole trader running a wedding hair and make-up business called **Elle Au Naturel**. From May to September she has at least one wedding every weekend and her cash flow is very healthy. During the winter months she has fewer weddings but has more hair and make-up trials. Clients pay a booking fee for the trial and if they wish to book the company for their wedding they pay a 10 per cent non-refundable deposit. However, Antonia found she still had to pay make-up artists for doing the trials and from November to April the business bank account was often overdrawn.

Her solution was to increase the client deposit to 50 per cent. This meant that she could afford to pay the make-up artists without going overdrawn. Even the brides-to-be preferred this arrangement as they had fewer bills to pay on their big day, so the solution was a great success for all involved.

Destocking

Having cash tied up in stock is a problem for many companies. With the use of bar codes, major retailers are able to operate a **Just-In-Time (JIT)** approach to their stock levels (this means they order only products they need, when they need them). The advantage is that they are not left with lots of unsold stock that they either have to sell at a loss (e.g. the reduced counter in Tesco for items about to reach their sell-by date) or throw away.

A company having cash flow difficulties can try to sell off stock to release cash to put into the business bank account and to make the bank balance more healthy – used car dealerships often do this at the end of the tax year.

> 'It is not the employer who pays the wages. Employers only handle the money. It is the customer who pays the wages.'
>
> Henry Ford

Revision essentials

EU grant: a subsidy available to new businesses which set up in areas of regeneration but there are conditions attached. In Helen and David's case they have to employ four EU citizens and are not allowed to sell the hotel for five years. They are also not allowed to use the property as their own residential dwelling.

USP: unique selling point.

Just-In-Time (JIT): a system designed to reduce cash tied up in stock – firms buy raw materials only when they need them and only produce goods to order, reducing storage costs.

Exercises

(20 marks; 25 minutes)

Read the unit, then ask yourself:

1 When facing a cash flow crisis a firm will often try to reduce cash outflows. How can it identify which costs to reduce? (2)

2 It will also try to increase inflows. Name two ways it could achieve this. (2)

3 Will increasing inflows increase profit? Explain your answer. (4)

4 Will reducing outflows increase profit? Explain your answer. (4)

5 Why do you think Helen and David found it so hard to reduce their costs? (4)

6 If you were the bank manager, what would you advise the couple to do? (4)

Practice questions

(20 marks; 25 minutes)

Dundee United players have agreed to postpone some bonus payments until next year to help the club's cash flow. The club are also issuing 13,000 new shares to generate £500,000 of additional cash inflow.

Chairman Eddie Thompson claims there is no need to panic. 'This is part of a three-year plan to bring in fresh income and ensure we stay financially viable,' he said.

But despite these measures there will be no more money for manager Ian McCall to spend when the transfer window opens in January. Instead if he wants to buy new players he will have to sell existing ones first.

Adapted from www.news.bbc.co.uk,
14 December 2004

Questions

1 What are the drawbacks of having to sell existing players before buying new ones? (4)

2 The club is selling more shares to generate more inflows. Discuss whether this is a good idea in the long term. (8)

3 You are the finance director for the club. Explain how you will improve its financial situation. (8)

15 How to improve profit

Multi-Michelin-starred Gordon Ramsay sharpened his knives and his tongue when, as part of the TV series *Ramsay's Kitchen Nightmares,* he visited a restaurant owner in crisis. In November 2004 the owners of **Momma Cherri's Soul Food Shack** had started talking about their options in the event of closure. If they didn't have a good December, then that was that. It's December 2004, enter Gordon Ramsay, the most feared and revered chef in Britain today, with his potent recipe of passion, perfectionism and inspirational leadership. Gordon had just one week to turn the business around.

Momma Cherri's Soul Food Shack

Momma Cherri's Soul Food Shack was a small 40-seater restaurant in Brighton. Owner Charita Jones was producing a menu of classic food from America's Deep South, but at the same time facing financial disaster. £65,000 in debt and with the punters missing, Charita was spending more and more time in the kitchen.

Ramsay loved the food and said her home cooking should be the restaurant's unique selling point. But Charita was killing herself trying to do everything and paying herself only £200 a week. She was paying two chefs, but there were hardly any customers: a surefire way to ruin a business. Ramsay's solution was for Charita to get out of the kitchen and start running the business properly.

Ramsay was confused about the menu prices: the restaurant was offering specials at £8 but on the menu dishes were a hefty £14. Why the leap? Charita said her bank manager suggested boosting prices to make money. Ramsay said it was killing the business. Charita needed to cut prices and offer smaller portions.

They let locals sample Momma Cherri food – and they loved it. Gordon overhauled the menu by offering a weekday £10 three-course menu of 'Soul in a Bowl'. The idea was to let customers sample small portions of different foods during the week, so that hopefully they would return on a weekend for more. But at £10 a head, Charita had to

> 'The measure of success is not whether you have a tough problem to deal with, but whether it's the same problem you had last year.'
> John Foster Dulles, US politician

fill the restaurant twice over each night to make it pay. It was a gamble that paid off: the customers loved the food, the front-of-house team pulled together and the vibe in the kitchen was professional.

Two years on, Gordon returned to find Momma Cherri now one of Brighton's biggest success stories. Charita had moved out of the shack to bigger premises round the corner. Momma Cherri's Big House has over five floors and is triple the Shack's size. People are booking up to four months in advance. There is an average of 900–1200 customers a week and it has become one of Ramsay's biggest success stories.

Adapted from: www.channel4.com

Improving profits

There are three main ways in which a business can attempt to improve its **profits**:

- by reducing costs
- by increasing **revenue**
- by expanding.

Reducing costs

Costs and profit have a direct effect upon one another. If costs are reduced then profits should increase. There is almost always some way in which a business can reduce costs. Momma Cherri found a way of cutting costs which allowed her to lower her prices, therefore tempting more customers into the restaurant.

1 Reduce workforce

A business could look to cutting the size of the workforce as a way of reducing costs. There are various ways in which it could do this:

- lose some workers and divide the extra work out among the remaining staff (do you think the remaining staff would be happy with this?)
- reduce the number of managers and cut a management layer out of the organisation (would the business be as efficient?)
- automate some jobs and replace people with machines (what would be the impact on the remaining workers?).

2 Contract-out the work

Many businesses today employ other firms to carry out certain jobs for them rather than employing someone full time. The most common example is with computer services – it is often cheaper to have a contract with a computer service company rather than employing your own staff.

3 Cut wages

Students often suggest that a business should cut wages. But this would have a devastating effect on staff – and all the high-quality ones would look for new jobs. One of the implications is that this could damage levels of customer service.

Reducing the workforce can be expensive. To automate jobs involves huge capital outlay to purchase the machinery in the first place; redundancies are hugely expensive. To keep redundancy costs low, many businesses rely on what is called 'natural wastage'. This means that organisations wait for workers to retire, or offer early retirement and then not replace them. The same would happen when a member of staff leaves; they are not replaced.

Increasing revenue

This means increasing income from sales.

1 Raise prices

Momma Cherri's bank manager suggested that she put up prices to increase her revenue. Raising prices is an option, but the success of this action will depend on the market in which the business operates and its competitors. Gordon Ramsay discovered that Momma Cherri's competitors all offered food at a much cheaper rate than Momma Cherri, so the action of raising prices actually meant that customers were lost. In theory a rise in price could lead to higher revenues, but only if it does not affect demand too much.

2 Increase sales

Gordon's approach was to attempt to increase the number of customers visiting the restaurant. Increasing sales volume is the more common way of attempting to increase revenues. This means, quite simply, setting out to sell more. Selling more at the same price, or even at a reduced price, means that a business can earn more. A business can use a variety of methods to attempt to increase the level of sales.

> *'There are three things you should spend your time doing: marketing, marketing, marketing ... if you are not prepared to do that then everything else is irrelevant.'*
>
> Emma Harrison, Entrepreneur

- **Advertising**: Momma Cherri went out and about in Brighton, offering sample food and advertising what she offered. She attempted to increase awareness of the product she was offering.
- **Sales promotions**: Momma Cherri offered a £10 lunchtime menu – it didn't matter how many people were at the table, the lunch would be £10. The idea was that while the customers were eating they would be buying drinks to wash down the food and this was where the money was being made. Other special offers include competitions or tokens. The important thing to remember is that the increased revenue must be more than the cost of the marketing.
- **Attracting new markets**: Momma Cherri's was only known locally; now it is a nationally known restaurant with people travelling from around the country to visit.
- **Reduced prices**: Momma Cherri reduced her prices to tempt customers into her restaurant. As a business becomes more popular and new customers are attracted, prices could eventually be raised with a hope that the new customers stay. A business needs to be wary of this action as it does not want to price itself out of the market.

3 Introduce new products

Based on Ramsay's advice, Momma Cherri launched a new product, 'Soul in a Bowl'. This strategy normally increases sales and in this case it did. Businesses often launch a brand new or updated version of an existing product as a way of increasing sales – often they want to be seen as modern and up to date. There are many customers who look forward to having the latest version of a product – do you know anybody who raced out to buy the latest HD digital TV or know someone who is always in the latest new fashions? Some industries regularly introduce new products: fashion, technology and car makers.

In all these cases the reason for bringing out the new products is to increase sales and gain a competitive edge. Businesses that do not regularly update their products or services risk losing out to their competitors.

Expanding

Momma Cherri decided to expand her business so that she could make more profit.

There are two ways in which a business can grow: internally, by increasing levels of production and sales, and externally, by taking over or merging with other firms.

If a firm is bigger it should in theory make more money. **European Home Retail** (EHR) was the company that owned **Farepak**, a food and gifts hamper business, sports outfit firm **Kitbag** and network marketing firm **Kleeneze**. The well-publicised collapse of Farepak in October 2006 should certainly highlight the dangers of expanding too quickly.

Following the collapse of EHR, home shopping firm **Findel** bought a number of EHR business assets, such as Kitbag and Kleeneze, in the hope that profits would grow automatically because of the firms' profits added together. Costs – such as administration, staff and purchase of supplies – can be cut, which should also lead to increased profits. Only time will tell whether Findel will do a better job than EHR.

Revision essentials

Profit: the amount of money a business is left with after paying all of its costs. It is the difference between revenue and costs.

Revenue: the amount of money earned by a firm from selling its products/services. It is calculated by multiplying the quantity of products sold by price.

Exercises

Read the unit, then ask yourself:

1 Suggest two reasons why it is important for a business to make a profit. (4)

2 Smith's Confectioners Ltd had the following costs and revenue:

Costs	Revenue
£2,318,000	£2,770,000

How much profit did the business earn? (2)

3 A new competitor has started operating and Smith's revenue has fallen by 10 per cent. Yet costs have remained the same. What is the new revenue? (2)

4 How much profit has the business earned? (2)

5 Describe two ways in which Smiths could increase its revenue. (4)

6 The Managing Director of Smiths has suggested using cheaper ingredients in an attempt to increase profits. Explain the implications of this decision. (6)

Practice questions

Pilgrims Frozen Food was in trouble. Pilgrims was a big distributor of everything from frozen pizzas to prawns. The company owed the bank £600,000 and could not pay. The business had gone bankrupt and the directors had left. The bank had appointed Buchler-Phillips as liquidator. It is the liquidator's job to raise as much money as possible from the sale of Pilgrims to pay the firm's creditors. The liquidator was going to try to sell the firm as a going concern and keep hold of the workforce.

The receivers eventually found a buyer for Pilgrims, Roy and Bruce Hodges. Roy and Bruce already owned Metrow Foods, a small local competitor of Pilgrims. They had outgrown the site they had been operating out of for 12 years, but buying Pilgrim's was a huge investment for them. Their main interest in buying the business was the premises, but they were also keen to see whether the business could support itself.

Combining Quality & Service

The Hodges managed to get Pilgrims back on its feet, but they were wary of the business's profits level and wanted to keep a check on its performance. Profits are still not what they should be.

Source: BBC, Trouble at the Top

Questions

1 Give two reasons why the profit levels may not be as high for Pilgrims as for Metrow Foods. (2)

2 Roy and Bruce have noticed that the costs for Pilgrims have been rising. Suggest two courses of action that they can take. (4)

3 Roy and Bruce wish to increase the sales revenue for Pilgrims and they do not have a lot of money to spend on advertising. Advise them of two strategies they could use, outlining the implications of each. (6)

4 Roy and Bruce are considering two options: merge Pilgrims Frozen Food with Metrow Foods and open more outlets in different parts of the country, or move into another area of the food market – fresh fruit and vegetables. Give two points in favour and two points against each of the two options. (8)

16 Break-even

Tushingham Sails Ltd manufactures windsurf boards in Blackawton, Devon. The company identified a potential market for a new design of windsurfing board. Everyone who has tried the board reckons it will be a success. A few magazines have reviewed it and have told the company to mass produce it. Tushingham will sell the board direct to customers through a website.

Before going ahead, Tushingham will have to make sure there is an opportunity to make some money out of the board. One way of doing this is to calculate the **break-even point**. The break-even point is the number of boards the company must sell to cover all the costs of making them. It is the point at which it is making neither a profit nor a loss. Tushingham will begin to make a profit once it sells more than this number. If it sells less, it will make a loss. Knowing the break-even level is important for any business.

Fixed and variable costs

> 'If you are failing to plan, you are planning to fail.'
> Tariq Siddique

As you studied in Unit 1, costs in a business can be divided into two types: fixed costs and variable costs. Before a business can calculate its break-even point it must first collect information about production costs. A business will need to know its fixed and variable costs and its sales revenue if it wants to be able to calculate its break-even point.

The fixed costs for the new board are £18,000. Rental for the premises, managers' salaries and loan repayments are all examples of fixed costs.

The variable costs are £200 per board. The raw materials, packaging costs, etc. all go up and down in line with the number made and sold.

Tushingham Sails has carried out some market research which shows that people are prepared to pay between £400 and £500 for a board. This helps the business decide on a selling price of £450. Knowing the selling price will allow Tushingham to calculate its sales revenue at different levels of production.

Tom, the Finance Director at Tushingham Sails, has summarised these costs:

Fixed costs = £18,000
Variable costs per windsurf = £ 200
Selling price per windsurf = £ 450

Drawing a break-even chart

It can be helpful to draw a diagram that shows the profit or loss at every possible level of output. This diagram is called a **break-even chart**.

To draw a break-even chart you need information about:

■ the variable costs
■ fixed costs
■ the revenue of the business
■ the maximum output of the business.

Tom will also need to know the following:

Total costs = Fixed costs + variable costs
Variable costs = Variable costs per unit × number of wind surfboards
Sales revenue = Selling price per unit × number of wind surfboards.

Maximum monthly production output of the factory is 200 units.

Stage One

Tom now starts to record the information on a graph. First he has to decide on the scales to use. For the horizontal scale (across), he needs to know the maximum number of windsurfs Tushingham is able to produce (200).

The highest figure on the vertical (up) scale is the maximum amount of money likely to be received. In this case, it is the maximum number of boards that can be sold multiplied by the selling price
200 × £450 = £90,000.

Below you can see the first stage of Tom's chart.

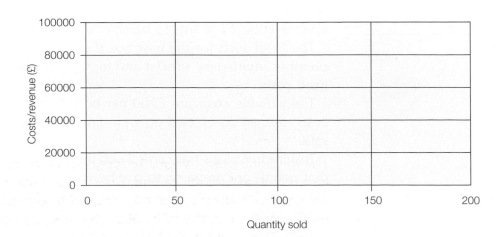

Stage Two

Tom needs to draw his £18,000 fixed costs line on his chart.

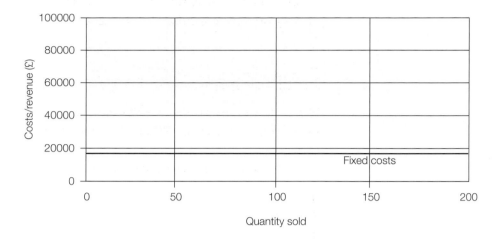

The line is horizontal because the fixed cost figure is the same no matter how many windsurf boards are sold.

Stage Three

Tom next needs to show the total costs. This means adding the variable costs to the fixed costs. If Tushingham sells nothing, its variable costs will be £0 (£200 × 0). If it sells 200 windsurfs, its variable costs will be £40,000 (£200 × 200). These costs however are on top of fixed costs. Tom must start the total costs line from where the fixed costs line meets the vertical axis. The gap between the total costs and the fixed costs shows the variable costs.

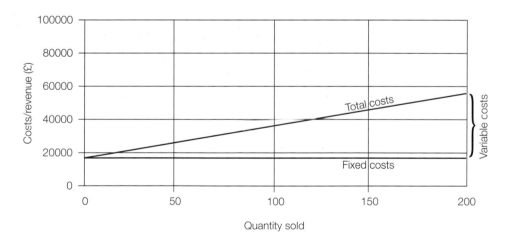

Stage Four

The third line drawn shows Tushingham's income from sales, the revenue. If no boards are sold, then no revenue is made (£450 × 0). So the line starts at zero. If all the windsurf boards that the company produces are sold, then £90,000 sales revenue would be received (£450 × 200). This is where the line should end.

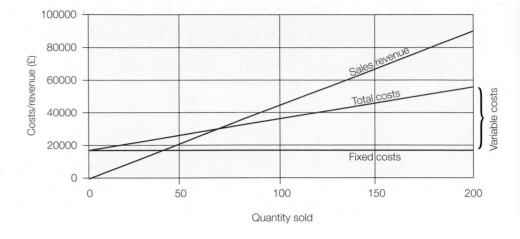

Stage Five

The point on the chart where the sales revenue line crosses the total costs line is the break-even point. Tom can now draw a vertical line down to the quantity sold and identify the number of boards the firm has to sell in order to ensure that all costs are covered.

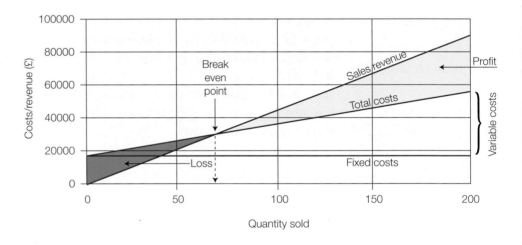

Tom reads the graph and can see that the line meets the horizontal axis at the number 72. This means that Tushingham needs to sell 72 windsurfs before it starts to make a profit.

The distance between the total cost line and the revenue line shows the loss which would be made at that level of sales. After the break-even point, the difference between the two lines represents profit. From the graph Tom can calculate that Tushingham will lose £18,000 if it sells no windsurfs, yet could make a maximum profit of £32,000.

Using break-even charts

Tushingham would be able to get other information from the break-even chart. Tom would be able to read off the graph the expected profit or loss to be made at any level of output.

Tom would be able to examine the effect on profit or loss of certain business decisions. For example, if a competitor brought out a similar windsurf and Tushingham needed to alter its prices, it could show the new situation on another break-even chart.

Revision essentials

Break-even point: the level of sales at which Total Sales = Total Revenue. At this point the firm is making neither a profit nor a loss. All output below this point is a loss. All output above this point is a profit.

Break-even chart: a graph which shows total costs and total revenues and the break-even point where total revenue equals total cost.

Exercises

(A: 15 marks; 20 minutes. B: 20 marks; 30 minutes)

A Read the unit, then ask yourself:

1 John sells hot dogs for a living. He calculates his fixed costs at £20 per day and his variable costs at 10p per hot dog. John sells each hot dog for 75p and is able to cook 50 hot dogs to sell every day. What are John's fixed costs if he makes and sells 25 hot dogs? (1)

2 What would John's variable costs be if he sold no hot dogs at all? (1)

3 What are John's total costs if he sells 20 hot dogs in a day? (2)

4 What would be the maximum sales revenue that John could take in one day? (2)

5 Explain what is meant by the term break-even. (3)

6 Outline two reasons why a business might want to be able to calculate the break-even point. (4)

7 Explain how to find the break-even point on a break-even chart. (2)

B

1 Toys 4 Fun is a manufacturer of children's wooden toys. The company has calculated the monthly costs of producing the average toy as follows:

Rent/Rates:	£2000
Electricity:	£100
Salary bill for managers:	£2700
Other fixed costs:	£200

Average variable costs for producing each toy come to £5.00. The average price for each toy amounts to £25.00. The factory's capacity is 300 units. Calculate the total costs and total revenue of the business over the following outputs: 0, 50, 100, 150, 200, 250, 300 (8)

2 Plot these figures onto a graph and estimate the break-even output. What is the profit/loss at the following levels of output: 100, 200, 300 (6)

3 If the company could not sell more than 150 in a month, what might the management do? (6)

Practice questions

Pride Hair Design is a Preston-based hairdressing salon, set up and run by Sue. It was partly funded by a bank loan on which there is an interest charge of £400 a year.

Sue is the only hairstylist. She allows herself £18,000 as a yearly salary. Roy keeps the accounts.

Sue has an assistant who works in the shop full time, doing jobs such as washing hair, sweeping up and answering the phone. Sue pays her £8000 per year. The average price she charges for all types of work, including OAP reductions, is £20.

Sue pays £5000 a year in rent and £600 a year in heating and lighting. It costs Sue 50p per person to shampoo and condition their hair. Other variable costs such as hair gel, hair spray, etc. cost on average £2 per customer. The maximum number of hair cuts Sue can do each week is 100. On average Sue receives 90 customers per week.

Questions

1 Identify Sue's fixed costs and variable costs. (4)

2 Using the information given, construct a break-even chart by carrying out the following tasks: (10)

On graph paper, draw and label the two break-even chart axes.

Draw the fixed and total cost lines and label them.

Draw in the revenue line.

Identify the break-even point.

Give your chart a suitable title and ensure the axes are labelled correctly.

3 From the chart, estimate the profit or loss if Sue had:

10 customers

70 customers

100 customers. (6)

4 Evaluate the potential success of Sue's business using the information you have. (5)

5 Sue thinks she could perhaps charge £40 per hair cut. Discuss the probable effect of increasing her prices to £40 per cut. (5)

Financing growth

All businesses start off small. **Subway** has 26,868 restaurants in 86 countries. It has 865 stores in the UK and Ireland and hopes to have 2010 by 2020. The company was started in 1965 by 17-year-old Fred DeLuca, who borrowed $1000 to open a sandwich shop. All he wanted was to raise enough money to pay his college tuition fees. He later became a billionaire thanks to Subway.

How does a company finance expansion?

Internal sources	External sources
Profit	Share capital/ increasing the number of partners
Sale of assets	Debt
Personal funds	Flotation on the stock exchange

Profit

Richard Branson began his Virgin empire at the age of 17 when he launched the magazine *Student.* His early venture was so successful that he used his profits to set up **Virgin**, a mail-order record company. Using profit means no interest will have to be paid but shareholders will get a smaller dividend and may be opposed to the expansion plans.

Sale of assets

In 1992 Richard Branson sold **Virgin Music** to **Thorn EMI** for £560 million to raise capital to support other business ventures, mainly Virgin Atlantic.

Smaller firms might sell off their buildings and then rent premises or may sell off computer equipment and choose to lease equipment instead. The main drawback is that while this can be an effective way of raising large sums of capital, it could cost the firm more in the long term. When Richard Branson sold off Virgin Music he sold the most successful and profitable part of his company.

Personal funds

In 1987 Richard Branson personally raised £200 million to buy out external shareholders and take back control of his business. This meant he could change the direction of the company as he saw fit.

Smaller businesses will not need to raise this type of capital. In 2005 Antonia Krieger expanded her wedding hair and make-up company **Elle Au Naturel** by creating a sister company and developing a new website. The investment needed was £10,000, a sum she raised herself by using the deposit she had saved to buy a flat. Using her savings meant she still lives in rented accommodation, but she has not had to pay any interest and if the expansion pays off she should soon be able to pay herself back.

Share capital

A limited company can sell more shares to raise finance for growth. The drawback is that the original owner may lose control. If it wasn't for the willingness to sell shares – especially on the stock market – the Sainsbury family would just be grocers instead of members of the super-rich.

When Richard Branson started Virgin Records he sold his friend Nik Powell a 40 per cent share in the company. This helped raise the funds needed to open the first retail store in 1971.

In 2006 more than 3000 new companies listed their shares on the London Stock Exchange.

Debt

A bank loan is probably the most common way a firm will finance expansion plans, but this comes at a cost – interest.

Helen and David Jones have financed their hotel in Andalucia by taking out a 25-year mortgage – they hope they will be able to pay the loan back sooner.

Flotation on the stock exchange

When Sumas, a Bristol-based financial advice company, wanted to expand by buying other businesses, it raised £3 million by going public and selling shares. It raised the funds needed for expansion, but the **flotation** cost £1 million and the business is now vulnerable to being bought up by a rival.

Revision essentials

External sources: sources of finance from outside the business, e.g. bank loan, venture capital.

Internal sources: sources of finance the company already has, e.g. selling assets.

Flotation: when a firm offers its shares for sale to the public for the first time on the stock exchange.

Exercises

(20 marks; 25 minutes)

Read the unit, then ask yourself:

1 A 20-year-old wants to start an aerobics gym. It will cost £60,000 to set up, but she has only £6500. Outline two suitable ways of raising the rest of the capital. (6)

2 A local double-glazing company is considering expanding its product range to include conservatories – it needs £300,000 to do this. Discuss the external options available to the company to raise this amount of cash and make a recommendation about what it should do. (9)

3 A local hairdresser has the opportunity to buy a second shop. Her family has offered to buy a 60 per cent share in her business – this will give her the money she needs for expansion. Or she could take out a loan. What should she do? (5)

Practice questions

(25 marks; 30 minutes)

In 2006 James Seddon appeared on BBC's *Dragon's Den* looking for finance for his water-free egg cooker. He had developed his design and had built a prototype. He believed there was massive potential in his product but did not have the finance to take the product from the prototype to the global marketplace.

His TV appearance did not go to plan and he failed to demonstrate that his invention worked, even forgetting to add the egg during his first demo! Despite this, two of the Dragons – Richard Farleigh and Peter Jones – invested £75,000 for a 40 per cent share in the company. Now the Eggxactly range of egg cookers is about to be launched, available for a single egg, two to six eggs or in an industrial version for the catering industry. The investors have yet to see whether they have made a wise investment.

Matt Hazell also appeared on the programme, hoping to raise £100,000 for a 5 per cent share in his technology company so he could market his invention, the Mermaid Pod. The Pod was designed for sailors. All the crew wear the device and when one falls overboard an alarm sounds and the device gives the skipper a grid reference to show where the crew member fell into the water. Richard Farleigh came up with the £100,000 but insisted on a 30 per cent share.

Questions

1 Appearing on a programme like *Dragon's Den* means an entrepreneur gets media exposure for his or her business while having the opportunity to raise money from a venture capitalist. What are the drawbacks of this? (6)

2 Why do you think James Seddon chose to appear on *Dragon's Den* rather than take a loan from the bank? (4)

3 Matt Hazell did not want to give 30 per cent of his business to the Dragons and tried to negotiate Richard into settling for 20 per cent. Why would Matt be reluctant to sell such a large stake in his business? (6)

4 Matt has come to see you before his TV appearance. Would you advise him to go on the show? Explain your answer. (9)

SECTION 4

EFFECTIVE PEOPLE MANAGEMENT

18 Organisational structure

Among your group of friends, is there a 'pecking order'? Is there someone who makes the decisions for your group or who tells the others what to do? You might have someone who is in charge, who makes the final decisions. You might have a newer member of the group who is always the person told to go and make the drinks! If there is, you probably have what is called an informal hierarchy within your group. Without this structure and defined roles you might never get anything organised and get to go for any nights out!

In businesses it is no different: they have structures too. For a small firm there may just be the owner/boss and a few staff working for him/her. In a large company, the structure will be more complex. It will help identify who does what job and who is in charge of whom.

An **organisation chart** is a pictorial representation of the structure of a business. Let's take the example of a small business employing five workers. The structure will be straightforward, as in the figure below.

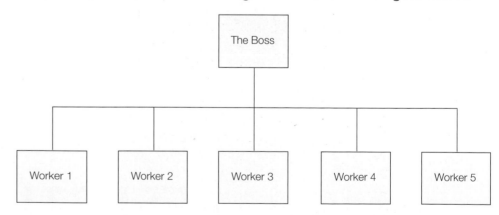

The chart shows that there is one person at the top of the organisation who makes all the decisions and there are five workers below who follow the instructions given.

Let's look now at the structure for a large organisation like the **Metropolitan Police**. The Metropolitan Police Service has a complex command structure that reflects its wide range of activities.

The purpose of the organisation chart is to show the hierarchy, chain of command and span of control within an organisation.

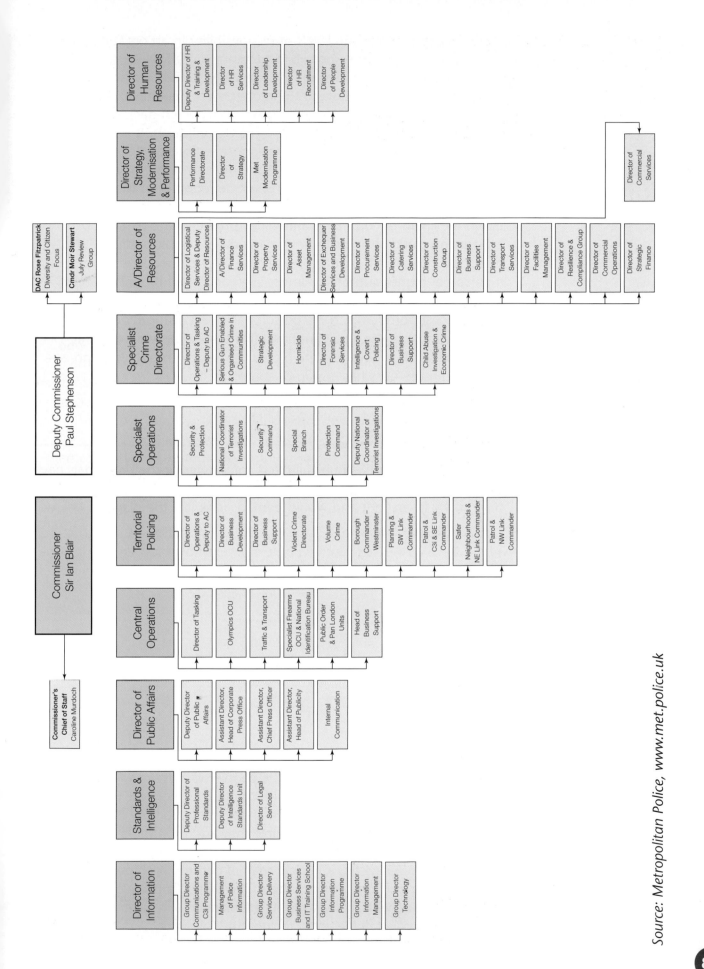

Source: Metropolitan Police, www.met.police.uk

Hierarchy refers to the levels of responsibility in an organisation. It is the formal structure of responsibility and authority and is usually shown in vertical layers. The further up the hierarchy somebody is, the more important they tend to be and the more power they have.

Chain of command refers to the route by which decisions are passed between the different levels in an organisation. It is the pathway of instructions and authority from the most senior people in an organisation down to the workers at the bottom of the hierarchy. A chain of command may be long or short depending on the organisation and the type of structure. Normally decisions are passed down the chain of command and issues/problems are passed up.

Span of control refers to how many other people someone is responsible for. A subordinate is a person who is directly responsible to a person of higher authority. Almost everyone in an organisation is subordinate to someone else. In other words, the span of control is the number of subordinates that a person has direct authority over.

The example of the small firm with five employees we looked at earlier showed two layers in the hierarchy; the chain of command is vertical and the boss has a span of control of five.

Tall structures

Large organisations like public limited companies or multinationals have more complex management structures. The organisation is likely to have many layers in it and would perhaps look like the diagram below.

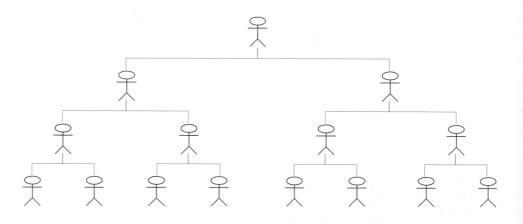

The chart is like a pyramid, with the people with the most responsibility at the top. The layers form a pyramid structure as there are fewer people at the top than at the bottom. The management structure has several clear levels of responsibility. The people they are responsible for are on the next line down on the chart. This structure is called a tall structure because the company has a narrow span of control: each person is responsible for only one or two others. The army is a really good example of a tall structure with many layers in the hierarchy.

Advantages of a tall hierarchy include the following:

- communication should be better because the chain of command shows a clear line for messages
- lots of opportunities for promotion
- it is easy to maintain standards across an organisation, since authority is strictly passed down the line
- it is easier to check everybody's work because there are managers and supervisors at each level.

Disadvantages include:

- the system is rigid and inflexible
- people's position in the management structure shows their level of responsibility and authority and it is often seen as a status symbol with clear divisions between managers and the workers
- there can be too many layers of management and this will create a long chain of command
- a long chain of command will mean it takes decisions a long time to reach the workers at the bottom of the hierarchy.

To overcome the problem of long chains of command, some businesses prefer a flatter structure, with fewer layers of management.

Flat structures

In a flat organisation each manager has a wider span of control. This means that each manager is responsible for more people. People on the lower levels have more responsibility than those on the lower levels in a tall organisation. Managers therefore need to have confidence in their staff. They also need to be happy delegating work to their subordinates.

'The best executive has the sense enough to pick good men, and the self-restraint enough to keep from meddling.'
Theodore Roosevelt

Advantages of a flat hierarchy include:

- fewer managers are needed, which saves money
- managers give more responsibility to the workers
- more responsibility leads to more job satisfaction for the workers
- there is faster, more efficient communication between staff and management
- it can lead to greater job satisfaction.

Disadvantages can be:

- each manager is responsible for more people
- managers have to rely on their subordinate staff much more to work efficiently and safely
- managers may lose control of subordinates as there is too wide a span of control for each manager
- it can lead to over-work and stress
- there are fewer opportunities for promotion.

Centralised organisations

Banks like **Lloyds TSB** and supermarket chains such as **Sainsbury's** are examples of businesses that are normally **centralised**. Local branch managers have little decision-making power: they are strictly controlled by head office and they have to follow the instructions they are given so that the branches operate in the same way. Managers are expected to send regular reports to head office. Head office will also arrange orders of supplies for all the branches; the branches have no control over finance.

Advantages of centralisation are:

- decisions can be taken with an overview of the whole company
- central managers are able to make sure that policies and decisions are followed consistently across the whole organisation
- decision-making and communication can be quick.

Drawbacks of centralisation are:

- it reduces delegation, which may lessen a company's ability to respond rapidly to changes in the market, since local managers have to refer to head office for decisions
- business opportunities may be lost because people are not allowed to make any decisions
- job satisfaction may be lost as staff are not able to feel involved.

'Management means helping people to get the best out of themselves, not organising things.'
Lauren Appley, www.businessballs.com

Decentralised organisations

A **decentralised** organisation is one that shares out the power of decision-making to more people. Important decisions are made locally at either the branch or division. Head office will make the policy and still have overall control but important decisions about the running of the branch will be made by the branch manager, for example. Flat organisations emphasise a decentralised approach to management as the structure encourages high employee involvement in decisions.

Revision essentials

Organisation chart: a diagram that shows the internal structure of an organisation.

Centralised organisation: an organisation in which most decisions are made at head office.

Decentralised organisation: an organisation which allows staff to make decisions at a local level.

Exercises

(30 marks; 30 minutes)

Read the unit, then ask yourself:

1 Outline the differences between a tall and a flat organisational structure. (4)

2 Identify the benefits to a business of having managers with a small span of control. (2)

3 Explain the implications to a large firm of having too many layers in its hierarchy. (4)

4 Name two examples of businesses, one that is centralised and one that is decentralised, and comment upon why they might have chosen to run the organisation in that particular way. (6)

5 a Draw an organisation chart to show the structure of your school. (5)

   b Give reasons as to why the structure is designed as it is and evaluate its effectiveness. (5)

   c Make suggestions for how the structure might be improved. (4)

Practice questions (40 marks; 45 minutes)

EduPlay is a medium-sized business located in a small town in Manchester. Sean and Rebecca Couzins set it up in 1986 after Sean lost his job with a multinational group. The experience of redundancy made Sean wary and this affected the way he chose to run the business. He wanted to keep total control over the management and finance of the company, yet establish an atmosphere of trust and cooperation between all members of the company.

The company sells educational toys for the pre-school child (1–5 years) and classroom toys for primary schools (5–9 years). The firm's policy had been to keep costs down and sell through both the internet and mail order, so there has been no need for sales people. The annual catalogue is sent to schools and playgroup leaders and small advertisements appear in the national weekend press.

In the organisation's structure there are only two levels: the Couzins and everyone else. The 48 employees are spread out as follows:

Production	24
Packing	15
Warehouse	5
Office	4

In the early days, workers were expected to cover each other's jobs when needed. This is still true, with all employees earning the same hourly rate. This situation has led to a number of complaints in recent months, since some jobs are seen to be 'easier' than others. The main grumble is that the equal wage for all isn't good enough. Another issue has arisen from the fact that the Couzins are in charge of decisions made in production, marketing, finance, personnel and design.

Several of the older employees have complained that as the firm gets bigger, the Couzins just don't seem to be in control of day-to-day events. Others have claimed that the Couzins leave jobs half finished and it takes for ever to get a decision made because there are so many demands on the pair. The secretary in the office commented that 'the left hand does not know what the right hand is doing'.

It seems clear that the organisation structure that was suitable for the company of the early days has now been outgrown and a change is needed if the company is to survive.

Questions

1 The Couzins are the only ones who can make any decisions, everyone is on the same pay and there are only two levels in the hierarchy. Outline why this might lead to problems in the running of the business. (5)

2 a Describe exactly how the current structure of the organisation might affect the following:

    the profitability of the company (4)

    the morale of the staff (4)

    communication in general. (4)

  b Take each of the above in turn and suggest things the Couzins might do to solve these problems. (9)

3 Explain how EduPlay should be structured. Use an organisation chart to illustrate your answer. (8)

4 Explain how these changes might improve the operation and success of EduPlay. (6)

19 Motivation

Why do people go to work? Is it *only* so they can earn money? Then why do some people volunteer to work on Christmas Day providing food for the homeless? They don't get paid, so what is it that makes them do it? A sense of achievement? There are many things that motivate us to do something. Why is that some people have a strong will to work and some don't?

Why do businesses need to know why workers work?

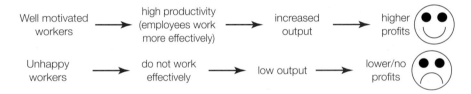

Motivation theory

There are several theories as to what it is that makes people work harder. The best known is Maslow's Hierarchy of Needs.

Maslow's Hierarchy of Needs

Maslow believed that **motivation** lies within individual employees. He divided human needs into categories and said that to motivate workers you must meet these needs. This was formed into a hierarchy of needs.

Maslow's hierarchy of needs

Once a lower-level need is satisfied, individuals strive to satisfy needs further up the hierarchy.

Application of the Hierarchy of Needs

When looking to motivate the workforce, managers need to think how to provide the opportunities to satisfy workers' needs. This is vital because a dissatisfied workforce will have high absenteeism and low productivity, whereas a motivated workforce can provide ideas for improving working methods, can put a smile on the face of customers and can provide the managers of tomorrow.

1 Physiological needs

The first needs that Maslow identified were physiological. Also known as basic needs, these include food, shelter and clothing. These needs can be met by financial means, giving the person the ability to feed, clothe and house their family.

Financial methods of motivation: pay.

- Time rate: this means that workers are paid for the amount of time taken to complete the job.
- Piece rate: workers are paid for how many items they finish. It is used to encourage workers to work faster in order to earn more money.
- Commission: commonly used in sales, the sales person is offered a basic wage plus commission – a percentage of the value of every item sold after the basic wage has been calculated.
- Performance-related pay: this is linked to the achieving of targets. If a worker exceeds the target, an extra bonus is earned.
- Perks or fringe benefits: one of the most common ways of motivating salaried staff is through fringe benefits or perks. These are extras, other than money, that the person may have in addition to his or her actual pay. Examples of perks are health insurance schemes, subsidised travel or accommodation, company cars and store discounts. It is often cheaper for the employer to provide goods rather than the money to buy them with. A good perk will make an employee reluctant to leave the business.

Maslow's hierarchy suggests that money is not enough on its own to motivate workers. Maslow felt that non-financial rewards acted as a better incentive for employees to work harder. Once an employee is earning enough money, they are seeking more than a financial incentive. Maslow's theory states that a worker could be earning a good basic wage but when this need is fulfilled they will then strive for more.

2 Safety, Security, Order

According to Maslow, people need to feel safe. They need to be sure that they are secure in their job. If their jobs are guaranteed, they can carry on meeting their basic needs and plan for the future. A business can fulfil this need by organising pension schemes, for example. The threat of redundancy is a big demotivator in this category.

3 Social needs

Maslow suggests that people strive for a sense of belonging – they want to feel part of a group or team. Businesses can attempt to satisfy this need by organising social events or clubs. Some firms organise social outings or family days for their employees. Businesses can also give their workers the opportunity to work in teams or take part in team-building exercises.

4 Esteem, Status

Businesses should allow their employees to feel respected and have a sense of status. It is therefore important for firms to recognise their employees' achievements and give them the chance of promotion.

Some jobs attract high status in society (nurse, vet, actor), while others are thought to be of low status (insurance sales person, window cleaner, street sweeper). Within a business, though, a good manager can make everyone feel important. The telephonist really is a crucial part of the team – so it is vital that the job is treated with respect.

5 Self-actualisation

This is the highest need that Maslow identifies. It is the satisfaction to be gained from challenging yourself to achieve more than you thought possible. It comes when you learn more about yourself and therefore can see yourself growing up into a new you.

Workers might get this from trying something scary and new – and then triumphing. The actor who has just done a love scene with a famous actress and did brilliantly. The sales person who has just made a huge sale to a difficult customer. This need can be fulfilled by someone doing an important job and taking responsibility.

Self-actualisation can come from both within and outside of work. Maslow believed that people always have the potential to set themselves ever greater challenges. A good manager keeps that in mind.

Advantages of a motivated workforce are:

- better productivity (amount produced per employee)
- better quality
- lower levels of absenteeism
- lower levels of staff turnover (number of employees leaving business)
- lower training and recruitment costs.

Conclusion

However large or small a business, the enthusiasm of employees, at all levels, can mean the difference between success and failure. People all have their own needs, drives, characteristics, personalities and contributions to make the business successful.

Revision essentials
Motivation: the will to work.

Exercises

(25 marks; 30 minutes)

Read the unit, then ask yourself:

1 Identify three reasons why people work. (3)
2 Describe what is meant by the term motivation. (2)
3 What is it called when workers are given perks in addition to their pay? (2)
4 Describe how Maslow's Hierarchy of Needs would motivate someone to work. (4)
5 Explain what needs you think would be met if you took on a paper round. (4)
6 How could an employer increase the amount of job satisfaction gained by its workers? (4)
7 Identify and explain three benefits that a highly motivated employee brings to a business. (6)

Practice questions

(25 marks; 25 minutes)

www.ristorantesalvatore.co.uk

Salvatore's is a restaurant chain in the North-West of England. Staff put in long hours and the work is hard. Salvatore, the restaurant owner, started out washing dishes and he's done every job in the business, so he feels that he can empathise with staff.

To attract the best staff and more importantly to keep them working there, Salvatore pays above the minimum wage. 'We're nothing without our staff,' he says. 'We wouldn't get customers leaving happy and coming back for more without them! We try to make all our staff feel that they are individuals.'

Salvatore even gives his staff cards and presents on their birthdays and at Christmas. He employs 80 staff.

Staff at Salvatore's are paid above average wages, work regular hours and there is a company pension scheme. And it's not just the practical benefits that Salvatore likes to give: 'There's a real family atmosphere in the company and that's down to the staff,' says Salvatore.

Questions

1 Identify three reasons why staff are important to a business like Salvatore's. (3)
2 Outline the benefits to Salvatore of a motivated workforce. (4)
3 Use Salvatore's as an example to discuss why money is not enough to motivate staff in the restaurant industry. (6)
4 Explain how Salvatore encourages people to work hard. Make reference to relevant theory where appropriate. (5)
5 Salvatore wishes to introduce some more non-financial methods of motivation. Discuss two methods that he could use, explaining the advantages and disadvantages of each. (7)

20 Communication

The importance of communication

Imagine it is a Saturday afternoon and a group of you have gone into town shopping. You go into Frockshop and decide to try on some clothes. A couple of you try on the same dress; they are all different sizes. The dresses are too small (no one admits this to the others, of course), but as you leave the fitting room you do mention it to the fitting room assistant.

Later on the same day more customers try on the dress; they also mention that the dress is too small. By the end of the week several customers have felt unhappy with the size of the dress and have made the same comments to various shop floor staff, yet none of the assistants does anything with the information – they decide it's not worth mentioning. Eventually the store decides to drop the dress from its product line due to poor sales figures. You start to shop at Lara where the dresses fit properly!

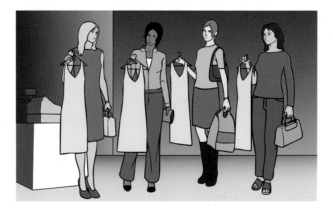

At Frockshop, the fitting room assistants were not involved in checking the quality or monitoring sales of clothes. Their job was to ensure the fitting room was run and managed well. The story would have ended differently if the store manager at Frockshop had taken the time to meet and talk with the fitting room assistants. She or he could have asked: which item of clothing has been tried on most today?

How many items that were tried on were then purchased? The store manager could then have discovered the problem: lots of dresses had been tried on, but none had been bought. The manager then would have been able to discover that in fact the batch of dresses was wrongly sized and faulty.

There are lots of different ways in which people can communicate. Even so, some businesses do not make the effort and take the time to communicate with all the staff within the business. Many employees in a business know and have an interest only in what their job is within their department. A really successful business will be one that communicates with its employees on a regular basis.

What is communication?

Communication is the passing of information between people. Good communication is the one ingredient which is essential for a business to become a success. Those firms that do not communicate with their employees will never run as well as those firms which communicate in full. The most successful companies are those that discourage one-way communication and encourage two-way communication – that is, from the people at the very top of the organisation right down to the people at the bottom.

One-way and two-way communication

One-way communication is when the receiver of a message has no chance to reply or respond to the message. An example would be 'I want you to write me an essay on motivation by Friday'. In one-way communication, the receiver, the pupil, does not get the opportunity to contribute to the conversation or communication, to ask questions or to provide feedback.

Two-way communication is where there is an opportunity for the receiver to give a reply or a response. This could be a discussion or confirmation that the message has been received and understood. This should lead to better and clearer information. An example would be a teacher saying 'I want you to write me an essay on motivation by Friday', then a pupil responding 'Can you explain what key points you want me to include', resulting in the teacher explaining the essay question further.

The advantages of two-way communication are that:

- tasks get done effectively and efficiently, with fewer mistakes
- it creates good employee relations – workers should feel valued and listened to by the firm.

A business that aims to run efficiently needs to be communicating at all levels.

Barriers to communication

Sometimes in businesses not all communication is effective. This is due to a variety of reasons:

- the person sending the communication might not explain themselves properly
- the receiver of information may not understand the message due to the technical language or jargon used
- the receiver may not hear or receive the message in the first place, e.g. a problem with the medium
- the message got distorted in its transmission (e.g. like a game of Chinese Whispers).

All these **barriers** would be overcome if there was an opportunity for feedback to clarify the message.

'The greatest problem in communication is the illusion that it has been accomplished.'
George Bernard Shaw

Effective communication

To be effective, communications need to be:

- clear and easily understood
- accurate
- complete
- appropriate
- via the right medium
- with a chance for feedback.

The process of effective communication

A business needs to make sure that it has effective communication channels to allow the flow of information around it. The communication process involves a sender, e.g. a 14-year-old boy; a message, 'Mum, can you come and pick me up?'; an appropriate medium, a text message; a receiver, Mum; and most importantly an opportunity for feedback, 'What time and where do you want me to pick you up from?'

It is not safe for anyone to assume that just because a message has been given it has been received and understood. Some big mistakes have been made as a result of poor communication. The infamous 'Charge of the Light Brigade' happened because the instructions of an army commander were misunderstood by his commanding officer. The result was nearly 200 men killed.

Information overload

Developments in telecommunications have had a real impact on the world of work. Information and communication technology (ICT) can

'The more elaborate
our means of
communication, the
less we communicate.'
Joseph Priestley,
philosopher

cut down the time it takes to send a message or information. Email and mobile phones mean that people can be contacted quickly. This should ensure more time to check that information has been received and understood properly, thus reducing the number of communication errors.

ICT can allow the same message to be sent to large numbers of people at once, for example using email. This could allow all the employees in a business to be kept informed of developments in the organisation, which could help to increase their motivation levels.

Advances in technology have meant that a person is confronted with lots of information every day – in emails, phone calls, newspapers, on radio and TV. With so many methods of communicating, sometimes people suffer from 'information overload'. This term was introduced by Alvin Toffler in his 1970 book *Future Shock*. A study ('Dying for Information') found that more than half of all managers were unable to deal effectively with the information they had to process. It can also mean though that some people in business are working 24/7, constantly being bombarded with information, and sometimes it is just too much for some people to cope with.

The purpose of communication

So why is communication so important to the success of a business? Managers need to communicate in a business in order to do the following:

- **Provide and collect information about the business**. The store manager in Topshop did not communicate properly with the shop floor workers and therefore a potentially profitable product line was dropped due to poor communication. Staff were not motivated to say anything. Managers will have no idea how the business is performing or what staff are doing without communicating.
- **Give instructions**. It is important that staff understand what jobs they have to do. Once a manager has planned how the business's aims and objectives will be achieved, the next job is to put the plans into action. All managers in all organisations need to give workers instructions as to what task they are required to do, who is to do the task and when it should be done by.
- **Ensure all workers are working towards the same goal**. It is very important that all workers have knowledge of what the company is aiming towards. A business might have a goal of achieving more profit. It might intend to achieve this by launching a new product. But if the research and development department and the marketing department do not know about this planned course of action, the aim probably will not be achieved.

Without managers having this knowledge, the business cannot run smoothly.

Poor communication

There are some key consequences of poor communication.

- **Misunderstandings**. Employees and managers may be given the wrong information and bad decisions could then be made.
- **Time wasted**. If the wrong message is sent or it is given to the wrong person, this can lead to time and money being wasted. Having to correct mistakes also wastes time and means jobs might have to be done twice.
- **Costs increasing**. Some mistakes could be costly. If, for example, the marketing department spends time planning a television advertising campaign but in fact only a radio advert is required, this would be very costly to the business.
- **Inefficiency**. Sometimes workers in a particular area of a business may have an idea which could improve efficiency – they may be doing a job every day and have a suggestion as to how the job could be done better. If there is no opportunity to communicate their ideas, this could cost the business money.
- **Low levels of motivation**. If staff feel that their ideas are not listened to, they might feel that they are unimportant and have low self-esteem, which could lead to decreasing productivity levels. If workers are constantly getting things wrong because instructions are not clear and they have no opportunity to clarify their understanding, this will lead to low motivation and perhaps high levels of staff absences.
- **Profits lost**. If communication within the organisation is poor, this is ultimately going to affect levels of customer service or sales – think of the Topshop example, where the customers turned to Warehouse. This will affect profits.
- **Disputes**. Poor communications between a business and its workers can lead to misunderstandings. In the worst cases this may lead to disputes and industrial action.

Revision essentials

Communication: the passing of information from one person or organisation to another.

Barrier to communication: something that prevents the flow of communication.

Internal communication: communication that takes place between people within the organisation.

External communication: communication that takes place between the business and people or organisations outside of the business.

Exercises

Read the unit, then ask yourself:

1 Use the chapter to identify four reasons why good communication is essential to any organisation. (4)

2 Give two reasons why a business might experience barriers to effective communication. (2)

3 Outline why it might be useful to a manager to give his workforce an opportunity to have a regular meeting about working practices. (3)

4 Explain two problems that could arise as a result of poor communication between the sales department and the production department. (6)

Practice questions

(15 marks; 20 minutes)

'The key thing I learned was the importance of good communication within any company. Without good communication on a day-to-day basis it can be very difficult to provide a good service.' A few years ago Pickfords' Removals Director Grant Whitaker spent a week on the vans in Birmingham to find out how he could make the business better. Pickfords is a nationwide moving and storage company.

All removals depend on the salesmen, who visit the customers first to price the job and see how long it will take before letting the removal men know what they think. More often than not the drivers arrive late to jobs and find irate customers waiting for them. However, it is not their fault as often they have difficulties getting furniture up and down stairs and out of the houses.

One of the drivers showed Grant a set of aluminium ladders he had found that would make lifting the furniture much easier and quicker, but head office would not listen to his idea. The drivers often feel they are kept in the dark about the business. Grant took his findings back to the board of directors for discussion.

Questions

1 a What evidence is there to suggest that there were poor communications at Pickfords? (4)

b Describe the benefits to the business of solving these problems. (4)

2 Explain the ways in which communications could be improved at Pickfords. (7)

21 Remuneration

Do you have a part-time job? How are you paid for the work you do? Most likely you will be paid for the hours that you work and you will receive this money weekly.

For most people one of the most important things about going to work is the amount they are paid. People can be paid in different ways, depending on the type of job and company policy.

There are two main methods of paying people for their work: **wages** and **salaries.**

Wages are usually paid to shop-floor and manual workers. They are normally paid weekly, sometimes in cash and sometimes into a bank account.

Salaries are usually paid to managers and office workers. They are usually stated at so much a year, although they are normally paid monthly. Salaries are paid straight into employees' bank accounts rather than in cash. People paid a salary are not usually paid overtime. They are expected to put in any extra time necessary to do the job.

'**Renumeration**' means all the financial rewards from a job – not only pay but also extras such as a company car or a pension.

Wages

Wages are based either on **time rates** or on **piece rates.**

Time rates

Workers are paid according to the time worked. Workers are usually paid a fixed hourly or weekly rate which can easily be calculated. The rate they are paid for a week's or an hour's work is their **basic rate**. This method does not depend on how much work the worker produces in the time worked. Time rate pay is often used for jobs where it is difficult to measure the level of output (the amount of work produced) by an employee. Workers will often have to 'clock in' or 'sign in' on arrival at work. In some organisations, if workers are one minute later than their starting time when they clock in, they lose fifteen minutes' pay. So it is important to get to work on time! This method of payment makes it very easy to calculate workers' wages and the worker knows exactly how much will be in their wage packet.

Time rate is criticised because it means everyone is paid the same whether they work hard and fast or not. Businesses need to employ supervisors or systems to ensure that workers are at work on time and work the hours they are supposed to. Workers also need to be monitored to make sure that they keep working and that a high level of work is maintained.

If the employee works longer than their normal hours, they will usually be paid **overtime**. This is the regular amount per hour plus an extra amount, perhaps time and a half. This system benefits employees as they are paid extra for any additional hours that they work. The offer of money is often a great incentive to encourage workers to put in longer hours during busy periods.

Example

The **Co-operative Bank** offers people £10 per hour to work as telephone customer advisors; these workers will be paid £10 for every hour that they work. The job requires the advisor to work 10am until 4pm Monday to Friday.

The Co-operative Bank also offers premium pay (overtime payments) for hours worked between 6pm and 8pm Monday to Friday and weekends.

Jan works five hours' overtime during the week for which the premium pay rate is time and a half. She also works four hours on Sunday for which she is paid double time. What would her wages be for that week?

Basic pay	$= £10 \times 30$ hours	$= £300$
Overtime, weekdays	$= £10 \times 1.5 \times 5$ hours	$= £75$
Overtime, Sunday	$= £10 \times 2 \times 4$ hours	$= £80$
Total pay for week		$= £455$

Take the example of the Co-operative Bank. Ask yourself, what are the implications of staff working so much overtime? Will they be tired? Will they still complete their job efficiently and effectively? Will they start to make mistakes? The impact of this could be great on a business like the Co-operative Bank. Will the same level of service be offered if Jan has worked a 12-hour shift or might she get grumpy with customers?

Piece rates

This means getting paid a certain amount for every unit of output or 'piece' made, i.e. the more you make, the more you get paid. Piece rate pay can be used only where the work of one worker can be counted or measured. This type of payment is normally used in factories, as it can be used only where it is possible to measure the performance produced by an individual or a team. It is also popular for work based at home, for example sewing and knitting garments, or packing and filling envelopes.

'You have to learn to treat people as a resource ... you have to ask not what do they cost, but what is the yield, what can they produce?'
Peter F. Drucker, management guru

Benefits of piece rate pay are:

■ workers work harder because the more they produce, the more they are paid
■ it is a fairer system than flat or time rate pay because diligent workers are paid more than lazy ones
■ people can work at their own pace if they want to. Some may prefer to work at a speed that suits them rather than be worn out going for higher wages.

But there are drawbacks of piece rate pay:

■ So that they can earn high wages, workers produce as many items as they can. This may result in poor quality work.
■ Firms have to spend more money on quality control.
■ Workers may also lose money, since they are not paid for work that is rejected or has to be corrected.

Payment by results

The more workers on a piecework produce, the more they get paid. It is a form of payment by results. There are also other forms of payment by results that are often paid in addition to workers who receive wages or salaries.

Commission. Sales people may be paid a basic salary, plus a commission (a percentage of the value of sales).

A & M Carpet and Bed Centre is a shop based in Wigan. Peter is the director of the business and is in charge of the day-to-day running of the shop. Tony is employed by the business as a salesman; he is paid a basic salary of £10,000 per year. Tony is also paid commission on every carpet or bed he sells; he receives 2 per cent of the value of anything he sells. What this means is that if Tony sells nothing he will still get paid the equivalent of £10,000 a year (roughly £833 per month).

If in one month Tony sells carpets to the value of £8000 and beds to the value of £2000, he will receive £1033 for that month.

How is this calculated? £8000 added to £2000 is £10,000; 2 per cent of £10,000 is £200; add this to the basic salary of £833 equals £1033. This means the more Tony sells, the more money he earns.

Bonuses. These are extra payments over and above the basic wage or salary. They are often paid as a reward for reaching a target. Bonuses are often linked in with piece rate pay; for example, if a worker produces more than their target they will be rewarded with a bonus.

The Co-operative Bank offers its staff a 10 per cent bonus if they reach their targets.

Performance-related pay. This is a payment for reaching an agreed target. It may be a personal target agreed with an individual.

Share option schemes. Some firms also allow their workers to have shares in the business. This can make employees feel part of the business and can give them an incentive to work hard because if the business performs better, this means more profits and, therefore, more money for the worker.

Fringe benefits

Fringe benefits are non-monetary rewards given to staff. Often known as 'perks', these are benefits other than money, paid in addition to wages or salaries. Examples include a company car, health insurance, payments into a pension fund, free life assurance, discounts when buying the firm's goods, shares in the company, use of a company mobile phone, subsidised canteen and leisure facilities.

Pizza Hut gives its workers a discount card to get money off their meals at the restaurant.

Freelance and temporary workers

Tony is the only member of staff employed by A & M Carpet and Bed Centre. Peter decided not to employ carpet fitters full time and instead makes use of freelance carpet fitters. They are not employed by the business, they work for A & M only when there is work for them to do. The carpet fitters charge £2.50 for every square metre of carpet that they fit and £3.50 for every square metre of cushion floor that they fit. This cost is added to the price that customers pay when they order a carpet.

Peter decided to use freelance carpet fitters because carpet sales are highly **seasonal**. Sales boom in the spring, but February is dead. If Peter employed the fitters full time he would have to pay them a set wage or salary and would effectively be paying them for doing nothing. By using freelance carpet fitters Peter has flexibility; he can use several fitters when the company is busy and use and pay for none when it is not.

It is a similar situation with temporary workers. Often businesses will employ people on a temporary or a fixed-term contract to help out when they might be busy or when permanent staff are on holiday. This type of work benefits both the business and the individual – the business is able to operate efficiently at busy times or when there could be potential staff shortages. The individual is able to perhaps earn extra money at expensive times of the year such as Christmas and does not have to make a long-term commitment to a business.

Revision essentials

Remuneration: all the financial rewards gained from work.

Wage: a method of paying employees for their work, usually on a weekly basis.

Salary: a method of paying employees for their work, usually calculated on an annual basis and paid monthly.

Commission: a method of payment where workers' pay is based on the value of products they have sold.

Piece rate pay: a method of payment where workers are paid per item or unit they produce.

Time rate pay: a method of payment where workers are paid per hour that they have worked.

Exercises

Read the unit, then ask yourself:

1 Outline the main difference between a time-based payment system and a salary payment system. (4)

2 Identify the difference between piece rate and a bonus. (2)

3 List five common fringe benefits given by companies. (5)

4 Identify which payment system might be suitable for each of the following jobs and briefly explain why: waitress, policeman, postman, manager, car assembly worker. (10)

5 Describe why businesses might offer workers fringe benefits. (4)

6 Explain how a results-based payment system works. (4)

7 a How much would Tony, the salesman at A & M Carpet and Bed Centre, be paid in a month if he did not sell anything? (1)

   b In January Tony sold £14,000 worth of carpets and £400 worth of beds. In February he sold £22,000 worth of carpets and £1000 worth of beds. How much would he be paid for each of these months? (3)

8 A firm agrees a performance-related pay scheme with its employees. If a firm's profits exceed £1.5 million, 3 per cent of the total profit will be shared between the 40 employees. If the business made £3 million that year, how much profit-related pay would each employee receive? (2)

Practice questions

St Helens Glass was established in 1970 and is a company that makes and fits double-glazing windows as well as other home improvement services. St Helens Glass employs just fewer than 500 staff in total.

St Helens Glass has a range of people working in various roles across the company. Senior management are paid between £50,000 and £60,000 per year. Senior management oversee the management of the whole operation. There are various levels of management, from junior managers whose salary starts at £20,000 per annum and middle managers who are paid from £30,000 per annum. All employees on the management team have use of a company mobile phone, use of the company gym and are part of a performance-related pay scheme where they receive a 5 per cent share of the total company profits that exceed £5 million. These staff are part of a share options scheme.

There is a sales team who are based around the whole country. They are paid a salary of £15,000 per annum and receive 3 per cent of any sales above £5,000 that they make each month as commission. They also have use of a company mobile phone and a company vehicle. These staff are also part of a share options scheme.

Of the 500 staff employed by St Helens Glass, 100 are production staff whose wages are calculated on a piece rate basis. Assemblers are paid 80 pence for each frame they make. These employees can also be part of the share options scheme.

St Helens Glass uses freelance window fitters to fit all its windows. The fitters are paid £2 for every window that they fit.

A team of cleaners is contracted to work various shifts. They are paid £5.20 per hour. The staff are paid time and a half if they work in excess of their basic hours during the week (four hours a day, Monday to Friday) and double time if they work at the weekends.

Source: adapted from www.sthelensglass.net

Questions

1 Jodie is one of the sales team. She sold £8000 worth of windows during February. What money will she receive in her pay packet at the end of March? (3)

2 Nick, one of the assemblers, makes 500 frames in one week. Calculate his gross pay for the end of the week. (3)

3 The table below outlines the hours of the cleaners who work at St Helens Glass. Using the information, calculate the three cleaners' pay for the week. (6)

Number of hours cleaners worked at St Helens Glass

	Karen	Catherine	Gary
Monday	8	9	9
Tuesday	8	8	9
Wednesday	8	8	0
Thursday	10	9	9
Friday	8	8	8
Saturday	3	0	4
Sunday	4	4	0

4 Discuss the advantages and disadvantages of St Helens Glass using freelance window fitters. (6)

5 Outline the reasons why a business like St Helens Glass would offer its workers non-financial rewards. (4)

6 Explain the benefits and drawbacks of St Helens Glass paying the assembly workers piece rate and the cleaners time rate pay. (8)

SECTION 5

THE WIDER WORLD

22 Ethics in business

Close your eyes and think of a petroleum company. Think of the profits it makes, the impact of oil upon the environment, disasters such as the Exxon oil spill back in 1990 that reportedly killed 250,000 sea birds, 2800 otters and billions of salmon and herring eggs (www.wikipedia.com).

Are your eyes still closed? Are you imagining an **ethical** company with a social conscience? I thought not!

What does it mean to be ethical?

'Ethics is a code of values which guide our choices and actions and determine the purpose and course of our lives.'
Ayn Rand, Russian-American novelist and philosopher (1905–1982)

All businesses have to follow **legislation** and failure to do so may result in their being prosecuted, but this does not include unethical behaviour. Being legal means operating within the law; being ethical means doing what is right.

If your school holds a non-uniform day for Children in Need and your friend turns up to school in non-uniform but does not pay their £1 for doing so, he or she hasn't broken a law but most people would believe he or she had behaved badly.

Ethical behaviour covers every aspect of business, including who a business buys supplies from, how it treats its employees, how it acts towards its competitors, the impact it has on the environment and the impact it has on its local community.

Ethical heroes

Who	What	Why
Total is a leading multinational energy company with 95,000 employees and operations in more than 130 countries. Total is the fourth largest oil and gas company in the world	In 2005 Total became the first company to sell **One water**. One water is a social enterprise which sells bottled water and donates all the profits to building roundabout-powered playpumps across Africa. As children play on the roundabout they pump fresh water from deep underground to a storage tank. The sales of One water in Total garages have already funded one playpump in the village of Ndondeni in Kwazulu Natal, South Africa	While a business may lose out on profit by behaving ethically, it gains considerably in positive PR. The side of the water tank paid for by Total has a board displaying the company's logo. The tank is in a remote village miles from anywhere; the people who live in the village don't own a car so the publicity is wasted on them. But Total can use that image in its marketing material. Being associated with a life-changing project provides a better image than the ones you had at the start of this chapter

> *'There's a hole in the moral ozone and it's getting bigger.'*
> Michael Josephson,
> American ethicist

But what about profit?

When behaving in a socially responsible way a business often has to put its money where its mouth is! Being ethical may mean being less profitable. One water donates all its profits to the charity and the founder Duncan Goose lives off a salary of just £12,000 (when he worked in advertising his salary was over £85,000). Other companies are making rather more money. At up to £1.30 a litre (£5.40 per gallon), bottled water is more expensive than petrol.

At the start of this chapter we were critical of oil companies and their behaviour. Yet with high petrol prices, do customers really care about the oil producers' behaviour, or do we just want petrol to be as cheap as possible?

Pressure groups

> *'Sharing money is what gives it its value.'*
> Elvis Presley

A **pressure group** can be described as an organised group that seeks to influence government policy, legislation and business behaviour. Pressure groups include **Greenpeace** and **Friends of the Earth** (environmental), **London Cycling Campaign** (a group which aims to make the city of London a world-class cycling city), **Amnesty International** (which campaigns for human rights) and **Searchlight**, which aims to combat racism and prejudice.

If a business behaves in a way that a pressure group disagrees with, the media may turn against the company. **Nike** suffered serious sales declines when its expensive trainers were revealed to be produced by low-wage Far Eastern factories. Pressure groups can embarrass companies and damage the company's image. This could lead consumers to boycott the business, damaging the profits and therefore upsetting the shareholders.

In 1999 **Shell** was decommissioning the Brent Spar North Sea oil platform and planned to dump it in the North Sea – it even had government permission to do so. However, campaigning by Greenpeace led to Shell dismantling the structure instead. Shell announced that this cost the company double the amount it had expected. But by working with environmental groups and changing its plans it improved its public image.

Pressure groups can also influence companies in other ways. We have already learned that a PLC sells its shares on the stock market and anyone can be a shareholder. In 2000 Greenpeace purchased £150,000 of Shell shares as part of its campaign to force the company to build a large-scale solar panel factory.

The FAIRTRADE Mark

Look for this Mark on Fairtrade products www.fairtrade.org.uk

When products display the **FAIRTRADE** Mark it means that disadvantaged producers in the developing world are getting a better deal. The producers have received a fair and stable price that covers the cost of sustainable production. In addition, producer organisations receive an extra payment, known as the Fairtrade social premium, to invest in social, environmental or economic development projects.

What this means is that when you buy a jar of Fairtrade certified coffee, the farmer who has grown the coffee has been paid fairly for his coffee beans and that money will be invested in community projects such as education and healthcare.

In 1994, when the FAIRTRADE Mark was first placed on products in the UK, Fairtrade retail sales were worth £2.7 million. In 2006 retail sales exceeeded £290 million and the UK is the largest Fairtrade market in Europe.

While most of us would agree that Fairtrade is a good thing, have you actually bought Fairtrade items and do you continue to buy them on a regular basis? Many people support the idea but are unwilling to pay the higher prices set by retailers for Fairtrade products. However, as more people demand and buy Fairtrade products, prices become increasingly competitive with conventional products.

Revision essentials

Ethics: a set of moral principles.

Ethical: doing things because you think they are morally right, e.g. refusing a bribe.

Legislation: laws passed by Parliament, e.g. The Sale of Goods Act, which says that goods sold must be fit to be used, or you can get your money back.

Socially responsible: acting in ways that show care and concern for all members of society, e.g. recycling waste materials.

Social enterprise: a business that trades in goods and services but is associated with a social cause, e.g Traidcraft.

Pressure group: a group with a common interest/goal who work collectively to further that cause, e.g. a trade union.

Fairtrade: a group that supports standards for importing goods from developing countries; they aim to ensure a fair deal for farmers and workers.

Exercises

(A and B: 30 marks; 30 minutes)

A   Read the unit, then ask yourself:

1 Explain in your own words what is meant by a firm being 'ethical'. (3)

2 Briefly explain the possible impact on its profit if:

    a A supermarket started charging 5p per plastic carrier bag (to cut down usage). (3)

    b A car manufacturer stopped producing 4x4 (petrol-hungry) cars. (3)

3 Google one of the pressure groups mentioned in the text. Outline two activities it has recently been involved in. (4)

4 Explain two potential benefits to a retailer of selling only Fairtrade items. (4)

B

The Co-op stores are built on a foundation of social responsibility, having developed from the co-operative movement started by the Rochdale Pioneers. In 1992 it became the first UK stockist of Cafe Direct products; in 1999 it made the decision to stock Fairtrade tea and coffee in all its stores; by 2005 it stocked over 100 Fairtrade products. Later that year the company won a prize for corporate social responsibility in the Annual Effectiveness awards.

1 Give two possible reasons for the Co-op making the decision to sell such a large range of Fairtrade products. (2)

2 How might achieving such an award help the Co-op achieve its aims and objectives? (5)

3 Should Tesco follow the Co-op's example? Explain your reasoning. (6)

Practice questions

(20 marks; 25 minutes)

CAFOD report: dire working conditions in computer production

A new CAFOD report, *Clean Up Your Computer,* exposes the dire working conditions in computer production in the developing world.

CAFOD has proof that electronic workers in Mexico, Thailand and China suffer harassment, discrimination and intolerable working conditions. The workers produce parts that end up in the computers of companies such as Hewlett-Packard, Dell and IBM.

CAFOD's Private Sector Analyst Katherine Astill said: 'The current situation is unacceptable. Its products may embody the latest in high technology, but labour standards in computer manufacturing can be appallingly low. CAFOD is campaigning for brand leaders to take greater responsibility for electronics workers. It wants Hewlett-Packard, Dell and IBM to adopt and ensure effective implementation of codes of conduct based on UN standards.'

Hewlett-Packard, IBM and Dell have seen the evidence and CAFOD has welcomed their initial responses to the findings and included them in the report. So far Hewlett-Packard has the best track record on labour standards, but all the companies recognise that more must be done.

Once employed, workers face long shifts on low pay in illegal short-term contracts that lack holidays, health, pension and employment benefits. One worker at an IBM factory said she was even refused time off when her father died.

One of the main problems is that workers face blacklisting if they complain. Days after three Guadalajara workers spoke to CAFOD about their treatment, they were fired.

The CAFOD report highlights an equally unacceptable situation for electronics workers in Asia. In Thailand, a worker making hard drives that end up in computers sold by companies like Dell earns around £2.50 per day. Michael Dell, the CEO of Dell, earned £134,000 per day in 2003.

Source: www.cafod.org.uk, 26 January 2004

Questions

1 The computer companies are not operating illegally because the working practices described above are not protected by law in those countries. Explain how they are behaving unethically. (5)

2 Explain how this press release issued by CAFOD may damage the companies included. (5)

3 You are a manager for Dell. How are you going to salvage this situation and try to make it beneficial to the business? (10)

23 Environmental issues

In November 2006 Uttesford Council rejected **Stansted Airport's** planning application to build a second runway due to concerns about climate change. This was the first case where fears about **global warning** have halted a firm's expansion and could have a huge impact on businesses throughout the UK. Stansted Airport is appealing against the decision.

How do environmental issues affect business?

Environmental issues can have both short-term and long-term effects on a firm.

In the longer term firms need to be able to overcome the challenge of global warming and resource depletion.

The threat of global warming is changing many businesses. **The Kyoto Agreement** means countries have pledged to reduce their CO_2 emissions. However, this can happen only if industry can reduce emissions but this could damage the economy.

American Electric Power is cutting CO_2 by investing in renewable energy projects in Chile. In Bulgaria it is changing school flat roofs to pitched steel roofs. These are all from recycled steel (discarded refrigerators, cars, building materials and other post-consumer products). From an energy viewpoint, standing seam metal roofs can bring some benefits to a school's energy budget. A pitched roof creates an attic space containing an insulating air pocket that helps control the amount of energy needed to heat and cool the building. Experts are also exploring ways to burn coal more cleanly.

Natural energy sources such as coal and gas are being used up and energy companies have to look at alternative fuels for the future. Electricity companies are anticipating growing markets for their wind power divisions and for more energy-efficient appliances. **General Motors Corporation** is spending millions to develop hydrogen-powered cars that don't emit CO_2.

Issue	Effect	Possible business response
Traffic congestion	Heavy traffic may mean customers won't make the trip to the business during certain times of the day	The business could change its hours by opening earlier and staying open longer. For example, the Trafford Centre in Manchester is open from 10am until 10pm during the week. The Trafford Centre is also working with public transport providers to make it more accessible. More retailers are operating internet shopping sites so people don't have to travel to stores
Noise pollution	Businesses found guilty of noise pollution receive heavy fines	Manchester Airport has paid for triple glazing for residents who live near the airport. It also has its own system for checking noise levels of aircraft taking off and fine the airlines if they break agreed noise levels
Recycling	The European Directive in Waste means that the UK must recover 60 per cent of all packaging waste by 31 December 2008. This means waste must be converted either into a usable form of energy or energy is made from the waste. This includes composting, and CHP generators operating from gases emitting from landfill sites	Offices use recycling facilities for printer cartridges, recycled paper, recycle their waste paper and cut down on power usage by turning off lights, etc.
Air pollution	Many small businesses pollute the air, e.g. Eddie Stobart lorries, power stations, etc. The law sets strict limits about how much air pollution companies can emit. Companies that break the law face hefty fines and a poor public image. But polluting the air can also damage people's health. Draft legislation proposes introducing a green tax on long-haul flights – at approx £27 per passenger this will increase air fares	Many transport companies are looking at greener fuels such as LPG and electricity to reduce exhaust emissions. Some new companies such as Future Forests have developed in response to this law and their website calculates the carbon cost of passengers' air travel and allows them to pay the company to plant trees on their behalf to pay back the planet
Water pollution	Companies which pollute rivers, streams, etc. are fined. This costs the company in lost profits and damages their image. Pollution can kill fish and other river dwellers and if it enters our drinking water can cause illness and death	Many businesses have reduced the use of chemicals. Organic farming, that is without the use of chemical pesticides or fertilisers, has increased. Waste chemicals from industry have to be disposed of properly

Global warming could change other industries, too. Many environmental scientists believe that even if we do reduce emissions the earth will still warm several more degrees in the next few decades. That could cut agricultural harvests, raise sea levels and bring more extreme weather.

For businesses, this presents threats – and opportunities. Insurers may face more floods, storms and other disasters. Farmers must adjust crops to changing climates. In the South of England, wine producers are having more success since their crop is now rarely affected by frost.

Some experts believe that the South of England could increase in temperature by 5 degrees. This would make it more suitable for wine than for wheat or apples.

Conclusion

Companies that launch low-emission cars, clean coal-burning technology or find cheap ways to reduce emissions will take over from those that don't move as quickly.

Revision essentials

The Kyoto Agreement: an amendment to the International Treaty on Climate Change; it has set compulsory targets for the reduction of greenhouse gases.

Global warming: the increased temperature of the earth's atmosphere and its oceans in recent decades that looks set to continue.

Food miles: a measure of how far food has travelled to reach the consumer's plate.

Carbon footprint: the measure of CO_2 (tonnes over a year) emitted by a business or individual through their consumption of fossil fuels.

Exercises

(20 marks; 25 minutes)

Read the unit, then ask yourself:

1 Polluting the environment doesn't just cost the earth – it can also hit your pocket. That's something Anglian Water knows to its cost. It was fined £190,000 after sludge from one of its sewage plants got into a river. It is one of the largest ever fines against a company. Explain why Anglian Water received such a high fine. (3)

2 This case was brought by the Environment Agency, a government body which checks that firms stick to environmental laws. Why do you think it is necessary to have this agency? Explain your answer. (5)

3 Outline how two different UK businesses might benefit from warmer temperatures in Britain. (6)

4 Explain how your school can change to become more environmentally friendly. (6)

Practice questions

Your Christmas dinner probably travelled 30,000 miles before ending up on your plate. A European turkey, African vegetables, Australian wine and American cranberry sauce will have notched up enough miles to circumnavigate the globe. Yet much of this produce could be easily acquired locally.

'There's simply no need to eat mange tout from Zimbabwe,' said Caroline Lucas, MEP for the Green Party. Ms Lucas, a member of the European Parliament's International Trade Committee and an MEP for South-east England, said thoughtless sourcing of produce was contributing significantly to the aviation industry's greenhouse gas emissions and the extension of 'monoculture' farming. She said: 'Ingredients for a traditional Christmas Dinner are in season in the UK right now – that's why they're traditionally eaten at Christmas.'

Author of a European Parliament report called *Stopping the Great Food Swap*, she added: 'African farmers are paying a high social and environmental price for switching traditional production to inappropriate cash crops geared for western markets, but seeing few of the financial benefits. By eating locally grown produce we can enjoy fresher, tastier food, support our local economies – and cut out some of the greenhouse gas emissions produced by the aviation industry as it flies all these vegetables around the world.'

The green cost of Christmas:

- 200,000 trees are felled to supply 1.7 billion Christmas cards sent in the UK
- 40,000 trees are used to make 8000 tonnes of wrapping paper used for presents
- nearly 6 million Christmas trees end up in landfill sites every January
- the UK throws out 3 million tonnes of extra waste over Christmas.

Adapted from news.bbc.co.uk, 25 December 2005

Questions

1 Some people argue that by buying our food from other countries we are helping the developing world. Others argue we should eat produce in season from the UK to reduce CO_2 from air traffic. Discuss whether we should buy only seasonal produce from the UK. (9)

2 The Chancellor is planning to increase taxes on airline travel in an attempt to offset the cost to the environment. Discuss the likely effects on:
    the airlines (4)
    supermarkets (4)
    other forms of transport (4)
    a small hotel in the Lake District. (4)

24 Economic issues

If you worked in a factory in the UK, how much do you think you would be paid? Around £6 an hour? It would depend upon the minimum wage, your skills, experience and what hourly rate competitors were offering you. Under EU law you would be entitled to regular breaks and a minimum of ten hours between shifts and annual holidays. A recent survey by the government found the median weekly wage in the UK to be £447.

However, pay rates vary enormously in Europe and around the world.

Country	Median weekly pay (£)
Brazil	£58
Bulgaria	£25
China	£23
Germany	£392
India	£15
Latvia	£46
Slovakia	£76

Source: © The Federation of European Employers (FedEE)

It is not too surprising, then, that many manufacturers in Britain are struggling to compete with foreign competitors. Not only do UK manufacturers have higher wage bills, but land costs are greater, as are transportation costs. Petrol prices are much lower in other countries.

Country	Unleaded petrol per litre
China	£0.19
Germany	£0.83
Latvia	£0.65
USA	£0.36
UK	£0.96

Source: AA Fuel Price Report, December 2006

It is little wonder that more and more manufacturers are relocating to Eastern Europe and Asia. They are taking advantage of cheaper wages and lower land costs in an attempt to reduce unit costs and remain competitive.

Good business sense or exploitation?

In December 2006 British Retailers **Tesco**, **Asda** and **Primark** hit the headlines with claims that they were exploiting workers in Bangladesh by paying as little as 5 pence an hour to people who were working 80 hours a week. All three retailers had signed up to a set of principles to provide decent working conditions and wages for workers in their supply chain, but the report claimed these were not being upheld.

A Tesco spokesman said workers at all its Bangladeshi suppliers were paid above the national minimum wage. Primark said its low prices were the result of good technology, efficient distribution, bulk buying and minimal advertising. Asda said it conducted 13,000 factory audits worldwide to ensure workers were not being exploited.

The Director General of the British Apparel and Textiles Confederation, John Wilson, said he believed British retailers were concerned about the welfare of the workers and were observing all employment laws. 'Clearly the level of wages seems very low to people in this country,' he said. 'But if it is the minimum wage that is being paid, which I understand is about £20 a month in Bangladesh ... as long as the audit is taking place at the factories, as long as all of the codes are being followed by all the people concerned – all of which I'm sure is happening in all of these cases – then at the end of the day, these are the circumstances in which these people are operating.'
Adapted from www.news.bbc.co.uk, 8 December 2006

'The first lesson of economics is scarcity: there is never enough of anything to satisfy all those who want it.'
Thomas Sowell, US economist, political writer and commentator

Import protection

Many countries try to protect home manufacturers by imposing import **quotas**. These limit the number of imported goods allowed into the country. This is an attempt by the government to protect home industry and employment. However, this reduces competition and gives consumers less choice. It also means the home producers do not have the same incentive to try to reduce costs or improve their products.

Farmers in the Isle of Man have had the advantage of import protection and will do so until 2011. The island can currently control meat imports because it is allowed to under special European Commission rules. This gives Manx farmers a much easier life than English farmers, who have to compete with French and other producers. At present, residents on the Isle of Man have a restricted choice of meat. However, the farmers have only until 2011 to prepare for increased competition when the protection stops.

Export subsidy

The EU doesn't just restrict the number of imported goods into the UK but subsidises home producers to export their products. Many EU farmers receive a **subsidy** for their crops, which enables them to compete on price across the EU and around the world.

The EU spends €1.7 billion a year supporting sugar prices. Five million tonnes of European sugar is exported to world markets every year. But under mounting pressure from the World Trade Commission, the EU is promising to reduce export subsidies and prices. This is bad news for sugar farmers who will find that without the EU subsidy they receive much less for their crops and will have to find ways of reducing costs, increasing production or switching to an alternative crop.

Revision essentials

Economist: someone who studies economics and writes about economic policy.

Scarcity: we have a limited availability of resources so cannot satisfy all of our needs and wants.

Quota: an import quota limits numbers of imports from foreign countries to protect home producers.

Subsidy: paid by the government to home producers to help keep prices competitive compared with foreign imports.

Exercises

(20 marks; 25 minutes)

Read the unit, then ask yourself:

1 Many high street banks have relocated their call centres to India to take advantage of lower wage costs. The NatWest bank however, has kept its centre in the UK. Outline two ways in which NatWest could use this situation to its advantage. (4)

2 Why do you think the World Trade Organisation objects to EU subsidies on farming? (4)

3 Outline two advantages to customers if the EU were to stop import quotas. (4)

4 Outline two advantages to retailers if the EU were to stop import quotas. (4)

5 Outline two disadvantages to UK manufacturers if the EU were to stop import quotas. (4)

Practice questions

(25 marks; 25 minutes)

In 2005 more than 75 million garments, including jumpers, T-shirts, blouses and bras, were held up in European ports because China had exceeded its quota on Chinese textile import quotas set by the EU.

Retailers warned of stock shortages and higher prices in shops if quotas remained in place. As things stand, quotas will remain in place until 2008, when they must end according to the rules of the World Trade Organisation. In the meantime, retailers are using their initiative to get garments out of China. The most popular is through Hong Kong, which remains quota free.

One clothing manufacturer employs workers in mainland China to cut out shirts, sew the hems, buttons or zips and then send the part-finished goods to Hong Kong. In Hong Kong, workers sew four seams connecting all the pieces together before sending the garment back to China for finishing, washing, ironing and packing. Producing a shirt this way costs 35–40 per cent more than if it was made in China alone.

Consumers are paying more for the fact that these are some of the best-travelled shirts you are likely to find. A single garment might travel up to six times across the border before it is finally shipped to the USA or Europe. Fortunately, western customers are willing to pay more for a shirt 'made in Hong Kong' than for one 'made in China'.

The process is complicated, time consuming and costly, but as long as quotas remain in place its popularity as a way of sourcing from China is likely to grow.

Adapted from news.bbc.co.uk, 5 September 2005

Questions

1 Explain why the quota system might lead to shops running out of stock. (4)

2 Why do you think British consumers believe a shirt that is 'made in Hong Kong' is better quality than one 'made in China'? (4)

3 The EU uses import quotas to protect EU manufacturers from the market being flooded by cheap imports. Explain how import quotas do this. (4)

4 What evidence is there in the text that import quotas are not working? (4)

5 Should the EU continue with import quotas? Discuss whether import quotas are a good or bad thing and give a recommendation. (9)

At the end of 2006 **Credit Action** announced statistics that the average UK adult has credit card and personal loan debts of £4056, with most adults having four credit cards. The average **interest rate** for credit card purchases is 15.75 per cent.

More worryingly, over 9 million people were refused credit by banks and other mainstream lenders. The **Citizens Advice Bureau** stated that its helpers saw over 1 million people about their debt problems. On average its clients owed £13,000 and it would take them 77 years to pay back the debt in full.

If you needed £350 to pay for a new central heating boiler but had been refused a loan by the bank, where would you go? Many people in the UK do not have bank accounts or savings, they have no credit rating and do not own their home. One company which will lend to these people is the doorstep lending company Provident Financial, which charges customers 177 per cent interest, making that £350 loan very expensive (you do the maths). While this rate of interest may seem astronomical, it is legal. Some doorstep lenders charge as much as 800 per cent (borrow £350 today, repay £3,150 in a year's time!).

The collapse of **Farepak** in October 2006 saw more than 100,000 people lose a total of £40 million in Christmas savings. This led to a government review of the collapse and many retailers stepped in to help the families. But the collapse of Farepak was an opportunity for doorstep lenders, some of whom wrote to Farepak customers offering them loans. This caused MPs to demand stricter regulation of the financial industry, including the setting of an interest rate ceiling. This would mean the government would be able to set maximum interest rates. If this regulation was to go ahead, companies like Provident Financial would find their profits badly affected.

This is just one example of how business in the UK is affected by laws. These can be set in the UK or in Europe.

> *'If you have ten thousand regulations, you lose respect for the law.'*
> Winston Churchill

Why have regulations on business?

There are many laws that govern the way a business behaves. If you and your friends went to a restaurant for lunch and one of your friends died as a result of food poisoning from their meal, you would expect the restaurant to be prosecuted. But if there were no regulations then standards in food hygiene would not have to be followed.

If you opened a hairdressers 300 yards from another salon you would expect them to compete with you for business, perhaps by starting a loyalty scheme or having some promotional offers. You would not, however, expect them to physically stop clients from visiting your salon, nor would you expect them to stop suppliers from dealing with you. Competition law ensures that competitive practices are fair.

When businesses recruit staff they are not allowed to discriminate on the grounds of gender, age, race, religion or disability.

The minimum wage

What is it?	Benefits to business	Drawbacks
The minimum wage was introduced in the UK in 1999 and guarantees an hourly rate of pay for workers. In 2006 the minimum wage was £5.35 for adults over 21, while 18–21-year-olds got £4.45 per hour. There are now campaigns for a higher minimum wage to be set for workers in London due to the higher costs of living in the capital	It encourages employers to train and develop staff by developing skills instead of relying on cheap labour. Higher pay reduces staff turnover, which costs employers millions of pounds a year in recruitment and training expenses. Better-paid workers spend their money locally, e.g. buying a sandwich on the way to work and a newspaper on the way home, thereby helping the local economy	Firms which do not pay their workers the minimum would be fined up to £5000. There were some concerns that small firms would not be able to afford to pay their workers the minimum and this would force them to make staff redundant

Health and safety regulation

What is it?	Benefits	Drawbacks
Regulations that exist to protect both the employees and the customers of a business. Some of the obvious things the law covers include providing employees with adequate heating and lighting, ensuring the workplace is ventilated and providing toilets and washing facilities	Many accidents in the workplace can be avoided. This would increase productivity, lower labour turnover (staff will want to stay in an environment where they feel safe and valued) and help the firm gain a good reputation. It will reduce the costs associated with work-related injuries. If the firm fails to follow these regulations it will be prosecuted	Often expensive to implement (special equipment, specialist staff). **Risk assessments** can be time consuming to carry out. Some staff resent the changes in working practices, as they see nothing wrong with how they have always carried out a job

What happens when things go wrong?

A head teacher from Derby was prosecuted for failing to alert his staff that the school had an asbestos problem. The windows were being replaced when the asbestos was discovered and this led to the school becoming contaminated. Asbestos has caused lung problems and cancer, so its discovery should have meant the school was closed.

In 2006 **Chester Zoo** was fined £25,000 and ordered to pay £50,000 in costs when it was found guilty of breaking health and safety laws. A zookeeper died after suffering a fractured skull when a 30-year-old female elephant, Kumara, struck the keeper on the head in February 2001. Shortly after the accident the zoo admitted Kumara had previously attacked another keeper twice. The prosecution had claimed there was an 'unreasonable risk of injury' generated by the zoo because there were no written protocols on the handling and training of elephants.

Since the ruling the zoo has changed its working practices to ensure such an incident never happens again.

Taxation

Government decisions about **tax** affect all businesses.

Tax	Explanation	Impact on a business
Corporation tax	A business pays this on its profits (usually around 30 per cent of the firm's profits)	This is deducted from net profit, meaning shareholders will get a lower dividend and the firm will have less to reinvest in the business
VAT (value added tax)	This has to be paid on goods and services at 17.5 per cent. Some items such as children's clothes are exempt	An increase in VAT would affect sales of some items like TVs or PCs
Income tax	A tax paid by employees on their earnings	An increase could lead to people having less money to spend on luxury items like holidays. A decrease in income tax would mean that people could afford more luxuries like holidays or a conservatory

Revision essentials

Interest rate: the charge for borrowing money and the reward for saving. High interest rates mean consumers will have less disposable income because their mortgages and car loans etc. will cost them more so they will have less to spend on other goods and services.

Discrimination: where one person/group of people is unfairly treated. People can be discriminated against because of their gender, age, religion, race, disability, weight, height, sexual orientation, etc.

Risk assessment: a process of identifying potential risks and steps that will be taken to minimise them. For example, on a school trip a possible risk could be a coach crash. Schools will attempt to avoid this by using a reputable coach company and ensuring all students wear seat belts.

Tax: a financial charge set by the government. Taxes are used to finance public services such as schools.

Exercises

Read the unit, then ask yourself:

1 Have you broken the law? In each case you must decide whether a law has been broken and explain your decision.

  a You run a trendy hairdressers in Covent Garden and are interviewing for a stylist. One candidate is an orthodox Jew who wears unusual clothes and has the typical hairstyle of his community. He has five years' experience at Vidal Sassoon but you worry he is not projecting the right image for your salon. Instead you give the job to a girl who has just finished college. (3)

  b A light bulb needs replacing in the coffee shop where you work. It is five minutes until opening time and while your manager has said that you must use a step ladder to replace the bulb, you climb on to a table instead so the job is quicker. (3)

  c John is a mechanic in your garage. After a holiday he returns to work dressed in women's clothing and asks everyone to call him Christine. He wants to use the ladies' toilet but your female staff object and you insist he continues to use the men's toilet. (3)

  d You are employing a new admin assistant who is Polish. As she is not British you pay her less than the minimum wage. It applies only to British people, doesn't it? (3)

2 You run a building company. How will an increase in income tax affect your sales? (2)

3 A leisure centre in Widnes had to be closed after it was found to have the bacteria that cause Legionnaires' disease in its water system. In this case no one contracted the disease. Thanks to health and safety guidelines, regular checks at the leisure centre had identified the bacteria and swift action by the council protected the public and the workforce. How did health and safety regulation prevent a crisis at this leisure centre? (3)

4 If the minimum wage is increased to £7, how is this likely to affect a small coffee shop? (3)

Andrea Winders and Tina Dutton from Warrington came up with a unique business idea back in 2005. Concerned with safety and the rising numbers of complaints from young women who did not feel safe travelling home alone after a night out, they saw a gap in the market for a taxi service that was available only for women – with only women drivers. However, due to the rules and regulations surrounding the taxi industry, the women soon realised they would be unable to go ahead with their original plan.

Pink Ladies, which has a women-only policy on drivers and passengers, is run on a members' only basis to avoid sex discrimination laws. Women who would like to use the service have to first become members (at a cost of £1). Because the cars (pink Renault Kangoos with luxury pink leather interiors) do not carry cash, members pay by using their account cards. They can top these up through the website or by telephoning head office. This means if a woman's handbag is stolen she can still get home safely. All drivers are trained in first aid and self-defence.

The service has been hugely popular and is already franchised in Carlisle and St Helens, with plans to open a further 30 franchises. But the expansion plans have been halted due to a new government road safety law, which means the company cannot operate its service without a licence. The Pink Ladies claim they do not need the licence because they are a members-only service, not a taxi firm. Becoming a taxi firm would mean it would have to employ male drivers under sex discrimination law.

Tina and Andrea are determined they will not be beaten and are taking their fight to Parliament.

Questions

> *'Bad laws were made to be broken.'*
> Doctor Who

1 Explain how Andrea and Tina could be breaking the law. (4)

2 Why may the government be right to be concerned about the safety of their service? (4)

3 Warrington taxi firms have welcomed the new legislation. How would they benefit from the forced closure of the Pink Ladies service? (4)

4 Should the service be allowed to continue or should the Pink Ladies be closed down? Justify your decision. (8)

Index